T

Love: Dark Night and Living Flame

and

The Glory of the Infinite

KENNETH WAPNICK, Ph.D.

Foundation for A COURSE IN MIRACLES®

Foundation for A Course in Miracles®
375 N Stephanie St, Suite 2311
Henderson, NV 89014
www.facim.org

Printed in the United States of America

First printing, 2025

Portions of *A Course in Miracles* © 1975, 1992
Psychotherapy: Purpose, Process and Practice © 1976, 2004
The Gifts of God © 1982
used by permission of the Foundation for Inner Peace.

ISBN 978-1-59142-961-6

Love: Dark Night and Living Flame

St. John of the Cross

Everyone has a handout, I assume, with the two poems on it. (See pages 96-98) That's where the title of the workshop comes from: "Love: Dark Night and Living Flame." These are two poems of St. John of the Cross. He's another of my favorite people that I'll be talking about. Let me just start by giving a brief history of John and who he was, and then situate these two poems in terms of his work. And then how they relate to what we'll be talking about today and some very important themes in the Course.

John of the Cross is a very famous Spanish mystic of the sixteenth century. His dates were 1542 to 1591. He actually is one of the greatest Christian mystics. In some sense, you can almost call him "the mystics' mystic." When you read him, you really know that you're in the presence of the real thing. He became a Carmelite monk in his twenties. He was ordained a priest.

Shortly afterwards, he met Theresa of Avila, who was about twenty-seven years older than he was. She was a Carmelite nun. She was in the process of trying to reform the Carmelite Order making it more spiritual and less worldly. She enlisted John's help because she recognized in him that he was the real thing, as he recognized it in her. They became very good friends. And they basically shared the same kind of spirituality that's reflected in their writings.

There was a lot of political stuff happening in the Church at that time, as is always happening in the Church. There was a movement in the Carmelites not to reform. One night, they took John from wherever he was staying, and they imprisoned him, and they tortured him, and they tried to force him to denounce the reformation. Not the Protestant Reformation, but the reformation of the Carmelites, and he refused. They

1

kept him in prison for nine months and he escaped. I have read a lot about John, and nowhere does it say how he escaped. Somehow they just say miraculously he escaped. He was in a very, very small cell and under conditions which were pretty awful. While he was there, he wrote one of his greatest poems—that's not what you have here—called *The Spiritual Canticle*, which is about forty-some-odd verses. And he wrote thirty-one of the verses while he was in prison. He then escaped and he rejoined Theresa, and he did a lot of work.

He was very well known as a spiritual director. He was very highly thought of. He was a very kind and gentle man, and people really wanted to talk to him about their problems, their spiritual journey, etc. And then he died in 1591. He's best known for his poems and his writings on his poems. I don't know Spanish unfortunately, but his poems are wonderful in English. They're supposed to be even more exquisite in Spanish. He's regarded as one of the finest Spanish poets.

He basically wrote three major poems: the two that you have on this sheet and *The Spiritual Canticle,* which all reflect his own mystical experience and his own experience of union with Jesus and with God. As was the custom in the Carmelites at that point—it was a custom that Theresa of Avila began—people would write poems and share them with each other as a way of joining and helping each other on their own spiritual journey.

When people read John's poems, they didn't know what the hell he was talking about. And so they asked if he would write about it. He then did a line-by-line exegesis of his poems, and these are the greater bulk of his writings. When it came to "The Dark Night," he never got past the second stanza of the eight stanzas. He did complete his work on "The Living Flame of Love" and he did write on *The Spiritual Canticle.*

2

His commentaries basically form the bulk of his writings on mysticism and spiritual development. He was a very, very holy man and, obviously, when you read his work, you know that he was not talking from his head. He really was talking from his own experience. He's best known for the phrase "the dark night of the soul," which I refer to a lot. Although strictly speaking, he never actually used that phrase. He talked about the dark night as you see in this poem. He talked about the dark night of the senses, but I don't think he ever used that term, although it's clear that's what he's talking about.

What he emphasized in his writings, which is basically only hinted at in these poems; you don't get any of the real detail, of course, is that one does not attain one's experience of love or one's experience of Oneness with God without a lot of work and a lot of journeying through what he referred to as the dark night. In this sense, as a student of the Course, you'll be very familiar with that idea that you don't get to the light until you go through the darkness. We'll discuss that a great deal more later on.

He was very clear about that. He was also very, very sharp, very, very intuitive, when he worked with all these nuns and monks who were professing to have these wonderful mystical, spiritual experiences. John recognized that these were really not the real thing. One does not decide one day to have an experience of union with God, and the next day have it. He did not use the term "ego," of course, and he certainly didn't have the kind of psychological sophistication we have today, but he certainly had it intuitively.

He recognized the tremendous struggle involved in letting go of oneself, which you find expressed a little bit in these two poems. The spiritual journey was really coming to grips with oneself, one's attachments to the ego thought system; although, of course, that's not his phrase, and then letting all that go.

He's perhaps best known for the single word "nada," which is the Spanish word that means nothing. Since he was a Carmelite, the image that he used was ascending Mt. Carmel. In fact his first major work, which began as an introduction to his analysis of the dark night, was called *The Ascent of Mt. Carmel*. As one makes one's way up the mountain, one must divest oneself of all worldly attachments, which we would then understand as being all ego attachments. So that there is nothing left of your ego. When you get to the top of the mountain, there's nothing. There is not a Bible; there is not a Catholic Church. All there is, is that experience of love. That's what "nada" means. In a sense, you negate everything that's not of God. And what's left is of God.

John, therefore, is part of a very rich tradition that you find not only in the West, but also in the East that the Course is also a part of. That's the tradition that you negate what is not of God, and what is left is of God. In other words, you look at your ego; you let go of your ego. You let go of your attachment to the thought system of the ego, of individuality, separation, guilt, specialness, attack. And what's left is the Love of God. That's how one makes one's ascent up the mountain.

I'll go through these poems with you and when you read John, you have to recognize that he's a creature of his culture. He was a sixteenth century Spanish Catholic monk. So Christianity, of course, was very, very important to him. He knew his scripture backwards and forwards. Clearly he gave it a spiritual interpretation, but he was very Catholic. Jesus was extraordinarily important to him

He was also an accomplished artist, and there's a very, very famous drawing of his of Jesus on the cross. When you look at the drawing, you can almost feel Jesus bursting off the cross, in a sense, being free of it. He did not believe in suffering for the sake of suffering. He believed that suffering was an inevitable part of letting go of one's ego.

That's probably enough about John as a background. Of these three poems that he wrote, *The Spiritual Canticle* came first while he was in prison at Toledo. The second was "The

Dark Night," and the third major poem was "The Living Flame of Love." He wrote many other poems and he had a lot of other incidental writings, but these three are his major achievement.

"The Dark Night"

"The Dark Night" is eight stanzas. We aren't going to do a line-by-line thing. Anyone who is interested, just get a hold of a copy of John of the Cross's work. He's the best commentator on his own work. Now let me also mention, because a little bit later I'm going to read some of Helen's dark night poems. In Helen's dark night poems, as she's writing them you get the clear sense that she's experiencing them.

What you find in "The Dark Night" is *after* the fact. In other words, John's looking at the dark night from the viewpoint of someone who has already passed through it. In Helen's poems, as you'll see when I read them with you, you get much more of a sense of the anguish of being in that darkness without any sense of light anywhere. Now again, that's implicit in what John is talking about. When he comments on the poems, he elaborates on that. But in the poems itself, you don't really get that feeling. Again, he's writing about the experience after it has happened.

So for him, the darkness wasn't a negative thing because it was a way to get to the light. And again, what he's referring to, especially when we look at his poems from the perspective of *A Course in Miracles*, is the darkness of looking and getting to the bottom of one's ego and recognizing the abyss that the ego thought system represents. So the poem begins:

> **One dark night,**
> **Fired with love's urgent longings**
> **- ah, the sheer grace! -**
> **I went out unseen,**
> **My house being now all stilled.**

What he means by his "house being now all stilled" is his ego; in that he has now quieted his ego self, and that's the darkness. His going out unseen is that he's unseen by the ego. He uses words in the next stanza of being secret and not being known. He has now left the ego. The ego is like a stranger to him; where he is now is a secret to the ego. What's very important, I think, is that second line, "fired with love's urgent longings." That's what allowed him and allows all of us to make this journey, is some awareness there's something on the other side.

You need to have an awareness that there's a point to all this struggle. That there's a point to dealing with the horror of the ego's system and all the angst that's associated with it: the tension, the fear and the guilt, and the hate and the self-hate, and the depression and the despair. If you don't have a sense that there's a purpose behind going through that, then it's hopeless. Then suicide is the only reasonable alternative.

What John is talking about is that he's "fired with love's urgent longings." He knows there's something beyond the darkness. And indeed he will not get to the light without going through the darkness. One won't get to the love without going through the hate. As we have seen over and over again, those of you who have heard me speak before; that's such a major theme of the Course. One does *not* get to the love unless one goes through the hate.

There's a passage in the text, where Jesus talks about how the Holy Spirit will lead you through the circle of fear, and God is on the other side (T-18.IX.3:9) So there has to be some recognition that there's a purpose behind this madness of dealing with one's ego; let alone dealing with other people's egos. And it's that fire that burns inside. It's that light that shines that leads you forward. And as we'll see a little bit later on, it's not an external light. It's something that you feel inside that gives a purpose and a meaning to your life.

God knows, there's no purpose in this life here. The only purpose in this life is not to be alive. The ego's purpose is to keep us from our true nature and our true Self. The only real purpose is the Holy Spirit's correction purpose, as it were, which uses the world as the vehicle or classroom for getting us beyond the world. It's that understanding that allows you to get through the daily process of working with this material. This course forces you, just by its very nature, to look at your ego, to look at the darkness. You bring the darkness to the light. You bring the illusion to the truth, which is *not* possible if you don't look at it.

You can't magically turn it over to the Holy Spirit and say please take it from me. You have to look at it with Him. That's what Jesus means in the text when he says, "Together we have the lamp that will dispel it" (T-11.V.1:3). *Together we have the lamp that will dispel the ego*; which means with him, we look at the ego. Together we look at the ego, as he explains at the end of that passage, so we can move beyond the ego. We look at the darkness. We go through the darkness so we can get beyond it. And it's that love that calls us.

There's a line in the workbook I always love to quote that says: "Our Love awaits us as we go to Him, and walks beside us showing us the way. He fails in nothing. He the End we seek, and He the Means by which we go to Him" (W-pII. 302.2:1-3*). Our Love awaits us as we go to Him, and He is the end we seek.* He's the reason we are on this journey, but He also is the Means by which we come to Him. In that particular lesson, God is meant for Love. But you can also understand that in terms of Jesus or the Holy Spirit. That's the goal. It's Jesus' love that we want, and yet it's his love which takes us to that love. It's the love that encourages us to continue so that we find the love.

The second stanza basically is like a repeat of the first:

In darkness, and secure,
By the secret ladder, disguised,
- ah, the sheer grace! -
in darkness and concealment
my house being now all stilled.

7

Again, this is just an elaboration of what we have just seen. The secret ladder is a secret because it's outside of the ego. That's what he means by it. We descend into the night, which is letting go of the ego or as he refers to it other places, the dark night of the senses. Basically we no longer are attached to anything external, which, in the Course's language, we understand means we are no longer attached to our special relationships. And it really isn't the form. It's not the behavior. It's the thought system that we project outside. When we divest ourselves of the darkness, it very quickly gives way to the light.

The ladder John described as being a ladder that both goes up and goes down as a ladder does. We both descend through the ego as we ascend to God. In a sense, the Course would use this same kind of analogy. Jesus often, like in the workbook for example, has us either sinking down into our thoughts to get past them to God, or we go up. Our thoughts rise up. Sometimes we go up; sometimes we go down. In a sense, John's doing the same thing with the ladder. The ladder goes up and the ladder goes down.

On that glad night,
In secret, for no one saw me,

Meaning I was all alone. I was detached from the world. That's what he's talking about. I was detached from the world. And again, the real meaning of this isn't that you are detached from anything specific, anything external or form. You're detached from the ego thought system. In other words, the ego did not see me because I had left the ego. I was no longer a part of that thought system. But as John frequently spoke about it, we then become no longer attached to anything external.

As you read him, however, it is clear that he's really talking about the content behind the form. Remember that he was also writing his books, his poems just came, as a means of instructing people who were coming to him for guidance.

He recognized that people were on all different parts of the journey. In fact he was very, very clear, which is what made him such a gentle and kind director that what you said to one person did not necessarily mean it was for someone else. He kind of criticized other people who would be guiding people on their spiritual journey who had steadfast rules: this is what you do; this is what the experience means; this is what you should not do. John said no one basically has the right to tell God how to lead you, and everyone is different. Everyone has different kinds of experiences and everyone needs a different kind of guidance and counsel. While he seems to be talking of letting go of external attachments, the real meaning behind that is letting go of the attachment to the ego *thought system* underneath. Because it's that thought system that keeps the Love of God away from us.

> **On that glad night,**
> **In secret, for no one saw me,**
> **Nor did I look at anything,**
> **With no other light or guide**
> **Than the one that burned in my heart.**

In other words, that there was no special person outside of me that was guiding me. The guidance really came from within. It was the Love of God that led John on his journey, and it's that same love that leads us.

That doesn't mean that there can't be external people who help us. But the way that they help us is they represent that love that's within us. Otherwise, it just becomes one more special relationship, just one form of idolatry. Anyone whom you look up to, if that person doesn't represent for you and help you reach that place of love and wisdom in yourself, then it just becomes another idol, which will lead you nowhere; which will keep you in the darkness instead of leading you through the darkness. Remember, for John, the darkness was a positive experience because it led you to the light.

> **This guided me** [this light that burned in my heart;
> this love that I felt within]
> **More surely than the light of noon**
> **To where he was awaiting me** [now he is the
> beloved, who is Jesus]
>
> **This guided me**
> **More surely than the light of noon**
> **To where he was awaiting me**
> **- him I knew so well -**
> **there in a place where no one appeared.**

In other words, this is not anything external. This is not a worldly experience. The top of the mountain is not a place. It's that state of mind in which there is no ego. There is no separation. There is no individuality. There is no specialness. All there is, is the Love of God. That light is more radiant and more clear than the light of the sun. What John is clearly expressing is that the journey is an inner journey, and that's what you trust and that's what you follow.

That's why I always caution students of the Course to stop making an idol of this book, because it's not this book you want to follow. It's the love that is the Source of the wisdom in this book you seek. Otherwise you end up worshiping the book or you worship a person who represents the book. The love and the wisdom in the Course is *your* love and wisdom, except you don't know it. It has to be externalized so you have something you can deal with. But the purpose is to bring you back inside.

We can rephrase that very important line that I always quote: this course is an outward picture of an inward condition (T-21.in.1:5). The original quote, as you know, has to do with the world and the inward condition is the ego. But if you restate it: this course is an outward picture of an inward condition; this course is an externalization; this course is a symbol of the inner condition of the love and wisdom that's in everyone's right mind. And that's what John is talking about.

He's not talking about an external experience. In his talking about the union of the soul with the beloved, he's basically talking about the union of the decision maker with the Holy Spirit or Jesus in our right minds. That's what he's talking about. Obviously this is a totally different culture. This is five hundred years ago or four hundred and fifty years ago, I guess. It's a different culture. It's a different age, but the content is identical. That's why John is still the mystics' mystic.

Q: He wasn't talking about going to his right mind so much as experiencing revelations?

K: Yes. Oh yes. Well, for him the union with Jesus was the union with God. He was a good Catholic monk, for him Jesus *was* God. And actually, as we'll see in the next poem, "The Living Flame of Love," he basically treats God, the Holy Spirit, and Jesus as one, because to him, they were one.

So yes, he's definitely talking about, in the Course's language, going to the one mind. At the top of the mountain, there's nada. There's nothing there. In a sense, again, in the Course's language, we would probably say that's the real world. But for John that was the acme of the journey—the summit of the mountain. There was nothing. There was nothing left but the soul's union with the beloved.

I was going to mention it in just a little while, but since we are already talking about it, the language, the imagery of John's poetry is, as it was for so many during this period, the imagery of "The Song of Songs" in the Old Testament for those of you who know that. It was attributed to Solomon, but actually it came much later than Solomon. The imagery is very sensual, if not sexual. And it's the union of the soul with the bridegroom. It is very difficult to be absolutely sure what the writer of those verses meant.

11

It can certainly be taken simply as a love song. It can also be taken as spiritual writers would take it, and as John certainly took it, as the union of the soul of Israel with God. Or actually John more specifically took it as the union of the soul with the Beloved. It's frankly love poetry—very, very beautiful—incredibly evocative. John took that imagery, again, just as many other writers did.

He also borrowed the Jesus references in the New Testament to the bridegroom, which you don't find here, but you certainly find them in *The Spiritual Canticle*; which is this wonderful interchange between the bride and the bridegroom: the bride being the soul and the bridegroom being Jesus. The bride in the canticle feeling at times that the bridegroom has deserted her because she can't find him, which we will actually find expressed very, very movingly in a couple of Helen's poems. Only to find that the bridegroom is always there, and really it was the bride who wasn't looking.

That imagery of the lover and the beloved is what's taken over here. This isn't meant to be a sexual thing at all. A psychologist could say well, this was the sublimation of John's repressed sexuality. But one could also claim, as Jesus would, that sexuality really is our repressed miracle impulses and our right-minded impulses. "You pays your money and takes your choice." But I think to read this as a sexual poem is really just a gross, gross distortion of what John was all about or the poems are all about. So again, on the fourth stanza:

> This guided me
> **More surely than the light of noon**
> **To where he was awaiting me**
> **- him who I knew so well -**
> **there in a place where no one appeared.**

He's talking about that secret place in one's heart. He's not talking about anything that's external.

From here on, it becomes much more rhapsodic and ecstatic. John now is basically expressing in verse the experience of that oneness and that unity with Love.

Oh guiding night!
O night more lovely than the dawn!
O night that has united
The Lover with his beloved,
Transforming the beloved in her Lover.

And of course, the ultimate goal is to be transformed to where you no longer are the individual person that you were, but you now are this—in John's terms, you now are the beloved. You now are Jesus. John would sometimes quote from the famous statement of St. Paul, "I live not I, but Christ liveth in me." That's what Christian mystics refer to as death to one's self, which we would refer to in the language of the Course as the undoing of the ego.

We become no longer identified with the ego. But we now become the manifestation of Jesus, just as he was the manifestation of the Holy Spirit. In other words, when one is in one's right mind, one then has no ego by definition. Therefore, one only allows that love to flow through. And when that love becomes permanent, and there is no ego left, that's what the Course calls the attainment of the real world. That's when you no longer vacillate between your wrong and right minds. That's when the ego is gone: when you have made a decision once and for all no longer to identify with it and its thought system. That's what John is referring to here where the beloved is transformed into the Lover. And again, the "night is more lovely than the dawn" because the journey through the ego has led one to the light. There was a purpose to the journey.

This is similar to the end of "The Obstacles to Peace." Jesus leads us on this long journey through the four obstacles. The final obstacle is the fear of God (T-19.IV-D). As we pass through that final veil, Jesus talks about how it's important to understand there was a purpose behind the journey. Without knowing there was a purpose, then you won't go through the journey because the journey will kill you, which is implied in the next poem.

The journey will kill you if you don't realize that there's a loving presence guiding you to that loving Presence that's beyond the veil. What that translates to in terms of one's personal work with the Course is realizing that there's a method in the madness, or what seems to be the madness at times in this course. Now it's the madness of looking at the ego's insanity. When you really begin to look at it, you delve into what seems to be a bottomless pit in your mind. It's like a cesspool of hate and of guilt and despair.

You don't get that so graphically portrayed here. It's talked about in John's commentary. You do get that in Helen's poems, which we'll look at in a little while. That's what we all try to cover over. That's why the world was made so that we wouldn't really confront this overwhelming, this awesome sense of guilt and self-hate that's inside of everyone.

The world is the cover. We then believe that there are things in the world that can give us pleasure and give us happiness and give us peace. And anything that is negative, we project the blame onto someone or something else. Anything not to confront the darkest of the dark: this dreaded tomb within our minds wherein dwells our most secret sin (T-31.VIII.9:2; T-28.V.7:5). No one wants to get anywhere near that. And yet it's only by going through that darkness that one gets to the light on the other side. It's only through going through this circle of fear that one finds the Love of God on the other side. It's only by going through the dark night that one finds one's beloved.

I've written about a series of experiences Helen had in my book on Helen (*Absence from Felicity*). It was like a waking vision; it was like a play because it had sequences. And it

began with the destruction of Qumran, and Helen seeing herself in a battered white dress, all soiled, and then making a journey up north to Galilee. There was a whole series of events, some positive, others negative. The end of the journey for Helen was in Galilee, which is very, very beautiful in springtime. Everything is all green. She saw this clump of trees like a forest. And then in the midst of the clump of trees, she saw a figure that she knew was Jesus. She started to cry and she said, "I never thought I would see those trees again."
That is what's at the end of the darkness. That's what is at the end of the journey. It's knowing that's what your goal is that enables you to make the journey, because this is a very perilous and difficult journey. That's what John is talking about. And again that's what he was guiding his people through. That's what Jesus is doing in this course. He's telling us this is not an easy journey. It ends up as the "journey without distance" (T-8.VI.9:7). Yet it ends up with nothing. It was nada.

But while you are in it, it doesn't feel that way because the ego is very, very strong. It's a very potent force, not because of anything within itself, but because of our belief in it. But what allows you to go through it is knowing that love is on the other side; that there's a sanity to all this madness.

Upon my flowering breast
[Now here again you see, this is the imagery of "The Song of Songs."]

Upon my flowering breast
Which I kept wholly for him alone,
There he lay sleeping,
And I caressing him
There in a breeze from the fanning cedars.

Again this is the kind of language you find in "The Song of Songs." What seems to be an erotic experience of love is really an expression in bodily terms of this love of the soul

15

for the beloved. Basically, as the Course says in the title of one section, it's "The Attraction of Love for Love" (T-12. VIII). It's the love within us that's attracted to the love that's still perceived to be external. So we personify it. We say it's God. We say it's the Holy Spirit. We say it's Jesus. In reality, it's really us. It's our unity of our selves with our Self. It's the decision maker finally detaching from the ego thought system and attaching to the thought system of the Holy Spirit, which ends up being our thought system. All the Holy Spirit is, is a memory of Who we truly are.

> **When the breeze blew from the turret,**
> **As I parted his hair,**
> **It wounded my neck**
> **With its gentle hand,**
> **Suspending all my senses.**

Let me just comment a little about this whole idea of a wound, because it comes up again in "The Living Flame of Love." This was a common mystical symbol. This is not a wound as we think of it as a wound. In the next poem, John refers to this as a cautery, which many of you may know is an instrument, like a branding iron that's used to burn abnormal tissue. It's a healing instrument. You burn away something that's unclean in oneself or that's damaged. It's a positive thing.

What this wound is that the beloved gives is that it suspends all my senses. In other words, it burns my ego. John referred at one point to the Old Testament statement about God that He's an all-consuming fire. In the positive sense of that, it's the fire that burns out the ego; not in a destructive way, but it just burns it up. Again, that's a common symbol both in the East and the West.

In Course language, we would say that forgiveness is the cautery that burns out our guilt. Remember, to our way of thinking, the Course is a much more sophisticated way of talking about the spiritual process. But the content that you find in the Course is no different than you find in any of the great mystics or spiritual teachers, East or West. You always want to get past the form to the content. You want to get past the symbol to the source. Otherwise, you will dismiss John or any great mystic as just a repressed sexual pervert, or something, without understanding that the language is only the vehicle he used or any great mystic used to express an underlying experience. This is no different from what the Course does.

Two hundred years from now, people will look at the Course and say, "Oh, it's quaint or it's this or it's that." There will be another set of symbols for another age.

Don't be taken in by the symbols and don't judge the symbols. Use the symbols as a way to get back to the source. The beloved's wound is what allows the lover or the soul to suspend the senses or get past the ego. And then what happens at that point is this wonderful final stanza:

I abandoned and forgot myself

In other words, I abandoned my ego and forgot who I was. There's another wonderful line at the end of a workbook lesson that says let me remember that myself is nothing and my Self is all (W-pII.358.1.7). The first self, of course, is spelled with a lower case "s" and the last one is spelled with a capital "S." *Let me not forget that self is nothing.* John would have loved that line. Myself is nada, is nothing. That's what he's saying here:

I abandoned and forgot myself. [*Let me remember myself is nothing and my Self is all.*]

One doesn't get to the true Self that is everything until one first looks at one's little "s" self, one's ego self, and says this is nothing. There's that lovely passage about the bridge to the real world. When we finally cross that bridge, the line says, we will awake in glad astonishment and realize for all this we gave up *nothing* (T-16.VI.11:4)! *For all this we gave up*

17

nothing! But on this side of the bridge, our self is everything. Our special attachments are everything. Our problems, our abuse, our victimization stories are everything. Whether it's positive or negative it's who we think we are, and we don't want to let them go. It's only when we finally let them go, we get to the top of the mountain; we cross the bridge that we realize this is all nothing. It was all nada. So that's what John is saying.

I abandoned and forgot myself,
Laying my face on my Beloved; [joining myself
now with the love that's in my right mind]

That was represented for John by Jesus, as it is for many of us. In this sense, it's no different from bhakti yoga, which is the practice of yoga that focuses on the love for the guru. John was very much a bhakti person as you can tell.

I abandoned and forgot myself,
Laying my face on my Beloved;
All things ceased;

Everything in the world ceased. All attachments to the ego thought system ceased. That doesn't mean you stop living. For example, in John's life, he was rather active. He was active in the reform for which he was punished, and he was active counseling people. He didn't spend his days as a recluse in his monastic cell. But what he means by all things ceased is all worldly attachments cease, all ego attachments cease.

I went out from myself,
leaving my cares
forgotten among the lilies.

Of course for us who are students of the Course, this is a wonderful, wonderful closing line, because lilies are the great symbol in the Course of forgiveness. All my cares, all my anxieties, all my worries, everything about my ego is now forgotten because they are forgiven.

**All things ceased; I went out from myself,
leaving my cares
forgotten among the lilies.**

All that's left is my union with the Beloved.

"The Living Flame of Love"

In the next poem, "The Living Flame of Love" which is only four stanzas, there's really no darkness at all. This is now John's expression of ecstasy. This is the last major poem that he wrote, and it really is about this living flame of love. What it feels like to experience this unity, this non-ego state, he can only hint at here. In fact when he commented on this poem, as he did his other poems; when he came to the final stanza, he just wrote one very short paragraph and basically said, I can't even speak of this.

Which, of course, you recognize is the same thing Jesus talks about in the Course. Every once in a while when he starts talking about God or what Heaven is, he breaks off and says, but there's no way you could understand this. Which is why there's really very, very little said in the Course about God. There's a lot said about what we do with God, but there's really very little said about the nature of God or the nature of Heaven, because as we are told right at the beginning, this is beyond what can be taught (T-in.1:6). But what can be taught is how to remove the interferences to our awareness of the presence of love or the presence of God. Well, in a sense, John would say the same thing.

**Oh living flame of love
That tenderly wounds my soul
In its deepest center!**

We have already seen what "wounds" mean. This isn't anything negative. This is the experience of burning away one's ego or losing one's ego or detaching from one's ego. And what allows us to let go of the ego is some awareness, some experience of love. It has to be something positive that allows us to go through this searing pain of one's ego. It's the awareness that there's something on the other side. Once again, if you do not believe there's anything on the other side, there's no point.

That's why in this course, which focuses so much on the ego, you also have all these other passages that point to what's beyond the ego. They can't be described, but we are always pointed to what's beyond the ego. We are asked to bring the darkness to the light. We are not asked to bring the darkness to the darkness.

The reason that the Course's *whole process of healing is one's relationship with the Holy Spirit or with Jesus* is because that's the light. They are the holders of the love. They are the symbols of the love that allows us to make our way through the darkness. Otherwise, again, there is no hope. That's why in the dark night of the senses, which John only alludes to here but it's certainly explained much more in his books, and certainly as you will find in other mystical literature and certainly what you find in the Course and will see it expressed in Helen's poems; that one's going through the darkness is very, very painful.

I mention this a lot, but there's no way of getting to the love unless you go through the pain. Many of you know the message I usually quote that Jesus gave to Helen and Bill, when he said it's so important that you recognize the intensity of your wish to get rid of each other (*Absence from Felicity*, p. 297). And then he went on to say you must get in touch with the hate. If you do not look at your hate for each other, you will never get to the love that's underneath. You must get through the hate, but you *can't get through it alone.*

The purpose of having a relationship with Jesus or the Holy Spirit is to have a guide who holds the lamp with you, who looks at the ego with you. Jesus can't do it without you, and you can't do it without him. That's what he means when he says remember that I need you as much as you need me (T-8.V.6:9-10). I need you because I can't help you without your help. You have to join with me. It's our joint hand that holds the lamp. Together we hold the lamp that will dispel the ego (T-11.V.1:3). It's that living flame of love that allows us to look at the ego and say, "I don't want this anymore." It's that experience that there's some truth behind all this illusion even if you don't experience it, but knowing that it's there.

Every once in a while almost every student of the Course will have some experience of light, some experience of hope. It may be very fleeting but it's enough. It allows you to know, yes, I have a right mind too. Now that's why it's so important that you understand that the split mind has two components to it. It has a wrong mind and a right mind. If you only know the wrong mind, which is what the ego wants us to only recognize, then there's no hope. Then there's nothing to choose between. So again:

> **Oh living flame of love**
> **That tenderly wounds my soul**
> **In its deepest center! Since**
> **Now you are not oppressive,**
> **Now consummate!**

This means I no longer experience your presence as oppressive. I am no longer afraid of the love. In a single line you have a tremendous wealth of information there. Actually this is what Jesus talks about in the Course. "Now you are not oppressive," and "now you are consummate." Now you are perfect. Now you are the end that I seek. You are now the fulfillment of my journey. Beforehand, you were oppressive. I didn't want the love. I was afraid of the love but that's not the case anymore.

One of the important things for students of the Course to always keep in mind is how much they *don't* want this course, and how much they *don't* want Jesus as their teacher, and how much they *don't* want the love that's on the other side. How much they *do* want to have a happier dream here. They don't want to awaken from the dream. It's really important to understand how much you *don't* want to awaken. If you don't understand the resistance, you can't let it go as Freud observed a hundred years ago.

If you don't know that you're resistant to therapy or to healing or to help or to love, then there's no way you will get beyond the interferences to them. It's important to understand that we find that living flame of love oppressive, because that's the end of who we are. We always want to keep it at arm's distance. That's when we worship Jesus as someone separate from us, as someone apart from us.

The point of John's poetry and his whole spirituality is to become one with Jesus, not to be seen as separate. He helps us become one with him, and in that unity Jesus disappears and we disappear, because at the top of the mountain is nada. There's nothing. You don't have a Bible. You don't have a savior. There's only that burning love; that living flame in which all individuality disappears. John wouldn't say it that way however, but it certainly is expressed. So again:

Since now you are not oppressive,
Now consummate! If it be your will:
Tear through the veil of this sweet encounter!

John mentions when he comments on this, making the same point Jesus does in the Course that it's important to understand that this is a veil, not a solid wall. We are taught in the Course that sin appears to us as a solid wall of granite that we can't penetrate; that we can't get through. But in truth, it's just a fragile veil that doesn't have the power to keep the light from shining through. That's what John is saying too.

Tear through the veil so there will no longer be separation. There will only be this unity, this burning of the living flame, because I'm no longer afraid of your love. I no longer find it oppressive. It is now the consummation of my journey. It's the consummate expression of who I am. It's what I yearn for. It's no longer what I'm afraid of. But remember again, John is writing these from the other side. He's no longer going through it.

Now he refers again to that symbol of the wound.

> **Oh sweet cautery,**
> **O delightful wound!**
> **O gentle hand! O delicate touch**
> **That tastes of eternal life**
> **And pays every debt!**

There's no way of understanding this from the poem, but in John's commentary, the wound is the Holy Spirit, the gentle hand is God, and the delicate touch is Jesus. And They are all One. That's the key thing. Again, it's this gentle wound, this delightful wound. It's this gentle hand that wounds us that undoes the ego. That's the meaning of the symbolism.

In the Course when Jesus talks about how we move beyond the body, he talks about how the body disappears and it's a quiet or gentle melting in (T-18.VI.14:6). The way the ego is dissolved is by this gentle melting in. You don't break it with a sledgehammer. You don't agonize over it. You don't fight it. You don't take out the bazookas and the tanks. There's a gentle melting in. It just gently dissolves in the presence of the flame of love. That's the wound.

> **O delicate touch**
> **That tastes of eternal life**
> **And pays every debt!**

What John means here is that it was well worth all of my suffering and all the trials and tribulations of the journey for what I'm now receiving. That's what he means that it pays every debt. It was well worth it.

In killing you changed death to life.

This is a reference of course to Jesus' death, but also to the death of the ego. In this wound that suspended my senses and undid my ego, there is now eternal life.

O lamps of fire!
In whose splendors
The deep caverns of feeling, once obscure and
blind,
Now give forth, so rarely, so exquisitely,
Both warmth and light to their Beloved.

Again these are the ecstatic outpourings of someone who has really experienced this union with love. *The deep caverns of feeling* we can understand as being the innermost recesses of our mind, which we now penetrate. Once they were obscure and blind. Once they were hidden in the ego's clouds of darkness: all the guilt and the hate and the despair and the fear. All that now is gone.

Now, what the mind *gives forth so rarely, so exquisitely, both warmth and light to their Beloved.* It's like when we get past the wrong mind, it's the love and the light of the right mind that just shines forth. Again, one does not get to the love unless one gets through the fear and the guilt and the darkness.

How gently and lovingly
You wake in my heart,
Where in secret you dwell alone;
And in your sweet breathing,
Filled with good and glory,
How tenderly you swell my heart with love.

That's why he couldn't comment on it. What do you say beyond that? This is what's beyond everything of the ego.

This is what *everyone* yearns for. This is what everyone who studies the Course yearns for. We would express it differently perhaps. But it's that unity of love, it's that experience of love that transcends all love here, transcends everything here, transcends all the special love and all the special hate. Over and over again in the Course, Jesus tells us what a shabby substitute we have made for the Love of God. The ego self and the body are parodies and travesties of the glorious Self that God created.

Over and over again he says if you only knew what lies beyond all this, you would rush to it. What he does in the Course is that he tells us there's something we want to rush to. But it's a journey that's treacherous and perilous if we don't take it with him or take it with someone who represents him; which again is what John was doing in his own work with the nuns and monks that came to him. This is not something that you can do alone, which is what he's saying here.

Questions

Q: Can John of the Cross's poem be compared to the Course's Lesson 109: "I rest in God," the birds chirping, the streams flowing?

K: Yes, yes. You don't have the kind of rhapsodic, ecstatic symbolism you have here. But yes, that's the end of the journey when you rest in God. Throughout the Course, as in that lesson, Jesus uses symbols of nature. You know, birds are chirping, brooks are flowing, and flowers are blooming. Just as John uses the imagery of "The Song of Songs," which is the union of the lover with the Beloved, the Course uses the symbols of nature. But they have the same meaning. Yes, it's the same experience. And, of course, you have in both poems the idea of resting with the Beloved. At the end of the dark night, I lay my face on my Beloved. And then here:

25

How gently and lovingly
you awake in my heart,
where in secret you dwell alone;
and in your sweet breathing,
filled with good and glory...

That's the same idea of resting in God, resting in Love. It doesn't matter what set of symbols you use. The content is the same. The experience of love is the same. Remember we live in a totally different age, a totally different culture. This is alien to us. When you read John, the language is alien. But when you read beyond the words, it's the same.

It's what Aldous Huxley referred to as the "perennial philosophy." There's a core experience whether you live in this century or twenty centuries ago, whether you are East or the West. There's a core experience because the mind is the same. Remember that the mind is timeless, not eternal, but it's timeless. It doesn't exist in time and space. It's the same hate and guilt, and it's the same love and peace. The right mind and the wrong mind never change. The forms of expression change.

While the forms of the expression are decidedly different now in our world than they were in the past in terms of the ego, the hate in the mind is no different now than it was one hundred years ago, five hundred years ago, two thousand years ago, three thousand years ago. Hate is hate; murder is murder; and love is love. And nothing ever changes. They don't change. The forms of expression change. That's what makes it possible to read a writer from another age and still benefit. You can read Shakespeare and still be uplifted and inspired even though the language is alien to us. And you can read John with the same experience. Actually he lived almost at the time of Shakespeare. He died a few years earlier. You get beyond the form to the content.

Q: When I read the mystics, the Catholic mystics mostly, it always seemed like a true mystic got there by the way of his or her religion. But what made him a mystic was that they left the form behind. That's why they very often said that once they had that experience that everything they had written before was straw or not worth anything. My question is would you classify somebody like Mother Theresa, a mystic, or was she not there? What makes somebody a mystic?

K: I don't know. I don't know enough about her, probably not. The word "mystic" is an awful word. I did my dissertation on mysticism, but it's an awful word because no one knows what the hell it is. People use it very, very haphazardly. Classically a mystic is someone who goes through what Evelyn Underhill called—an ordered movement where there is a sequence. There's a process, which culminates in an experience of Oneness with God.

I think that what makes someone an authentic mystic is that one takes that experience and then goes back into the world, so that it doesn't become like a private, selfish thing. The love just is shared. But I think to establish a category is really a mistake, because it then becomes something that is an "it." You know, have you gotten to "it"? Have you had the experience that makes you a mystic? And that's nonsense.

Q: The way I always understood the word was that a mystic was somebody who transcended the world. I never read about the definition or anything.

K: Well, yes, you can say that. In the Course, being in one's right mind would be in a sense a form of mysticism and being in the real world is the culmination of it. And that's the experience open to everyone. It's a word that had a reference in the past. But I think today we are too sophisticated for that hopefully. Again, it becomes a way of branding people and making people special. The whole idea is that everyone is an inherent mystic, because everyone has the same right mind. Everyone has the same Love of God that's in that right mind. So what do you mean by a mystic, except being in touch with that Love of God.

Q: Would you tell us how John got his name John of the Cross?

K: I mentioned it briefly but I didn't go into it. He was born Juan de Yepes. I don't speak Spanish as you can tell. Anyway, when he became ordained, he took the name John of the Cross—Juan de la Cruz. As I mentioned earlier, Jesus was extremely important to him and to be Catholic meant that the cross was important so he took the name.

Q: Do people, who in the course of this life time don't experience the pain, which I believe there are a lot of people who don't. Do they ever get motivated to change? To get to something like this?

K: In the Course process, the answer is no. Remember that the Course is only one path among many thousands, so that it's not the only path. Within its path, as it says near the beginning, that it's the pain that you feel that impels you to seek the other way. That's why there's that section which begins with the statement that the Holy Spirit wants you to know how miserable you are, because he can't teach you without that contrast. It's "The Happy Learner" section, which begins with talking about how miserable we are (T-14.II.1:1-3), because it's the misery that would impel us to make the journey and choose the right teacher for the journey. Within *A Course in Miracles* itself, the answer is yes; it's our experience of pain or the experience that nothing here works that would impel us to really seek the other way.

Q. Isn't pain also the inevitable result of dislodging ourselves from God?

K: Well, sure, when you dislodge yourself from God that is the ego, so yes. But it's only painful because the ego tells you that you've done it, because in truth you haven't dislodged yourself from God.

Q: But as long as you believe you have?

K: Yes, but once you believe in it, you're attaching yourself to the ego, so in a sense it's really part of the same thing.

Q: The pain comes in the resistance when we take the tiny, mad idea seriously. Because if we are at the point that we are aware it's only a tiny, mad idea, there would not necessarily be the pain. But when we start taking it seriously, because then there would be the absence of Source, the absence of Who we are, and that would be where the pain would be?

K: Remember that pain can't come from anything real. Pain can't come from separating from God because we didn't separate from God. Anymore than pain can come from something external impinging on you, physically or emotionally, because there's nothing outside of you and there's nothing in you to be impinged upon.

Pain comes when you identify with the ego that tells you that you separated from God, and that was a terrible thing. Pain comes from your believing that you're a body, and bodies mean that you're vulnerable. And when you're vulnerable, you'll get hurt emotionally and physically. But the pain doesn't come from anything that seems to have happened because nothing happens. Pain always comes from choosing the ego, which is the resistance to the truth, which is that there is no ego; we never separated. We are still at home with God and love is the only reality.

Q: The concept in the Course is Atonement without sacrifice, Atonement without pain, if we choose the Holy Spirit.

K: Yes, yes.

Q: Because all of this wouldn't be painful.

K: Right, and if we could have chosen the Holy Spirit at the beginning, and if we can choose the Holy Spirit at any given moment, there's no pain. The pain comes in resisting the choice, because we listen to the ego that says if you choose the Holy Spirit, you will destroyed; you will be devastated; you will be annihilated; you will disappear into oblivion.

·

Again that's what makes this course so simple, as Jesus says over and over again. That's the problem. That's why there's no order of difficulty in miracles (T-1.I.1), and no hierarchy of illusions (T-23.II.2:3); which is another way of saying the same thing because the problem is never what's out here. We always make up nonexistent problems and then try to solve them out here. And the problem is simply our listening to the ego and choosing to attach to its thought system. Once again, that's what John is talking about. He's talking about attaching to the ego thought system. When he talks about the dark night of the senses, he's really not talking about the senses. That's what the words are saying, but the content is the attachment to a thought system, and it's that thought system which is the defense against, or the resistance to the true thought system. That's where all pain comes from.

A "Course in Miracles–John of the Cross" Story

I thought I would just tell a quick *Course in Miracles'* John of the Cross story. This goes back in the very early days. Helen was still taking the Course down. They (Bill and Helen) became very, very good friends with a doctoral intern at the psychiatric institute, who was a priest. This is the famous Father Michael that we refer to. He was attending a supervision session with Bill. I wasn't there, and I forget exactly what Bill had said, but he was talking about a different way of looking at defenses.

Afterwards, Father Michael went to Bill's office and said; I don't know if you ever heard of him, but everything you just said in this class sounded just like St. John of the Cross. At which point Bill opened up his desk drawer and out came the collected works of John of the Cross. So anyway, that's *A Course in Miracles'* John of the Cross story.

I think what Father Michael was referring to and what Bill must have talked about was that the defenses really were not something necessarily pathological, which is how psychologists would talk about it. In other words, that's the be all and end all of them, but that there were ways of getting beyond the defenses themselves. That the defenses then could serve a right-minded purpose to get through the dark night to the light on the other side.

Q: What was last sentence you said?

K: The right-minded use of defenses. In other words, typically psychologists look at defenses and attack them. You know, there's this pathology and it means this, that, and the other thing. And what Bill was suggesting, which of course is what the Course is saying, was that since everything is a defense here, the right-minded way of looking at it is to see that it's something you choose to defend against the love that is in you. There's a line that says what the ego made to harm, the Holy Spirit uses to heal (T-25.VI.4:1). So, that's all.

Helen's "Dark Night" Poems; Introduction

I want to turn now to some of Helen's poems. I read a lot of Helen's poems as you know, but usually I read the nice ones. I don't usually read the dark night poems. So this is the opportunity to read some of those. She basically wrote four of them, and they really express what the darkness is in each of us. One of the ways that the dark night of the soul is frequently talked about, not only by John of the Cross, but by all spiritual writers, is that it's the period that directly precedes the final illumination.

In the teacher's manual, as you know, Jesus talks about the six stages in the "Development of Trust." The sixth and final stage is the attainment of the real world, which in the Course is a consummation of the process. The fifth stage is the worst of all of them. That's the one he says that you may remain in it a "long, long time" (M-4.I-A:7:7). The description of that fifth stage is when you totally give up all judgment in a way different from what you thought it was.

And that can certainly be translated to say, as I do, that that fifth stage is really when you give up all sense of self. The fourth stage, as you may recall, which is a very positive stage, is a stage of real peace. It's basically when you learn to forgive, and you realize that forgiveness works much, much better than attack and judgment or any form of specialness. But there's still in that fourth stage a sense of "I." "I" forgive. "I" have let go of my ego. There's a strong sense of self. In the fourth stage is when Jesus says you have not gone as far as you thought (M-4.I-A.6:10).

The fifth stage is when you suddenly realize what has to be let go of is not only the ego thought system of judgment and hate and specialness and pain, but the whole thought system: everything, the whole sense of "I," the whole dream. And that's the Course's equivalent of the dark night of the soul. It's in that period when you literally feel there's no hope; that love is totally absent; that God has gone off somewhere and Jesus is out to lunch. And it's a very long lunch and there's nothing to sustain you anymore.

Again John talks about that. Most spiritual writers talk about it as does the Course. This is what Helen is experiencing in these poems. The specific subject of each of these poems is Jesus. She feels that he has abandoned her, he has left her, and he has not kept his promises. And what you are left with, which is what makes these poems very evocative and very moving, is a tremendous sense of desolation and emptiness. It's beyond the anger. It's beyond the disappointment. It's beyond the hurt. There's an emptiness, and you'll see this in the poems.

I mentioned this very, very briefly earlier, when I also talked very briefly about *The Spiritual Canticle,* which is John's very large poem and magnificent poem, which is a dialogue of the bride and the bridegroom: the bridegroom being Jesus and the bride being the soul. The bride complains to the bridegroom, "Where have you gone?" And in a sense that's what Helen is doing here complaining to Jesus, "Where have you gone? You have left me, and I'm absolutely desolate."

My point in reading these to you, which we will talk about as I read them, is that this is what's at the heart of everyone's mind. This is the core of everyone's wrong mind. This is what we are desperately trying to deny. We build one layer of defense after another, one fantasy after another, one world after another, to try to keep this emptiness, this tremendous sense of loneliness and bottomless abyss of nothingness away, because it's so painful. Beyond the pain, beyond the hurt, beyond the anger and the rage is this.

"The Ancient Love"

Here's the first one. It's called "The Ancient Love" and in this Jesus was the love obviously.

Love, You are silent. Not one shining word
Has reached my heart for an eternity
Of waiting and of tears. I have forgot
Your face that once was everything to me,
But now is almost nothing. What You were
I do but half remember. What You are
I do not know at all. What You will be
Is unimagined. Sometimes I believe
I knew You once. And then again I think
You were a dream that once I thought was real.

My eyes are closing, Love. Without Your Word
I will but sleep, and sleeping will forget
Even the dream. Is silence what You gave
In golden promise as the Son of God?
Is this bleak unresponsive shadowland
The overcoming that You offered those

33

Who understood the Father through the Son?
Is endless distance what must stand between
My Love and me? You promised that You will
Forever answer. Yet, Love, You are still.
(*The Gifts of God*, p. 44)

This is again very, very painful. The point I made earlier
when I was talking about Helen's poems and John's poems,
is John's poems are written after the fact. They are written
from that point of love and that point of light looking back on
the journey. This is right in the heart of the journey. In fact,
this is what that fifth stage is (M-4.I-A.7). This is again where
everyone wants to avoid. Indeed that's what all special relationships are. They are an attempt to cover over this emptiness and this quiet stillness that's not peaceful. This isn't the
stillness of the still, small Voice of God.

This is the stillness of saying there is nothing: God is the
dream and love is the dream and Jesus is the dream and hope
is the dream. And it's all for naught. I think many students at
some point or another in their work with the Course will go
through that. This course held out a promise, and it failed the
promise. I have worked and I have worked and I have
worked, and I have nothing to show for it. My life is even
worse than it was. I don't hear anything. Before I thought I
heard a voice. Now I don't hear a voice. And the only voice I
hear is a voice of emptiness and stillness, and it is not a nice
voice. And, of course, there's the accusation of Jesus that,
"You promised, and is this what you promised me?"

Q: Ken, can I just ask about that one when she talks about
her memory of "I knew you once." Is she talking about her
lifetime now or more towards the images?

K: Well, I think so. Helen was kind of a strange person in
many ways. She had many kinds of experiences of past
lives—certainly a lot with Bill, some kind of veiled ones with
Jesus. But she stubbornly maintained to her death that she
didn't believe in reincarnation. That was typical of Helen.
This poem is a very personal poem and her experience of Jesus

was so personal. So yes, I think she was referring in some way to having known him when he was on this earth.

She had a psychic, whom she didn't believe in anyway, but she did go to a psychic. She was dragged to a psychic once in England, actually; Bill dragged her. She was a good psychic. She told Helen who she was—not a biblical figure, but the Bible is so notoriously unreliable—but that she was very close to Jesus. And the same psychic told her that she never got over the crucifixion. And that experience I mentioned earlier about Helen, beginning at the destruction of Qumran and then her going north to the trees in Galilee; that really had to do with Jesus as well. Somehow the emptiness and the destruction was in a sense all that was left of the promise. At least that's the context of it, so, yes.

"Prayer for a House"

This next poem is called "Prayer for a House." It is on page 49. It's a wonderful poem because of the evocative language of this kind of despair. It's not a very happy poem. It does have an interesting story however. This was actually written for Bill. Helen never wrote poems for Bill because she didn't like Bill. But Bill moved from his apartment on the Upper East Side to another apartment on the Upper East Side. I said to Helen, "You know it might be nice if you wrote like a housewarming poem for Bill." Well, this is the poem that came. It's an awful housewarming gift. I'm afraid I'm responsible for this poem. It's called "Prayer for a House," again, this is addressed to Jesus.

>Enter my house. Its holiness is Yours,
>And it must wait for You who are the home
>Of Holiness Itself. Its altar stands
>Darkened as yet, but open to the light
>That You will bring. I have forgot the glow
>Of diamonds and the glittering of gold

That once I thought would lighten up the dark
And bring me comfort. Silvered drapes are gone,

And floors are empty of the heavy rugs
That once concealed their bareness with designs
That Eastern hands had woven carefully
In thick obscurity. Their bareness is
The sign the Guest that was to come is yet
Not ready to appear, and bring the peace
That He has promised those who dwell with Him.
My ringless fingers hold a lamp long since
Gone out and cold. The wind sings bitterly
A chant of fear that echoes round the walls
And enters ceaselessly into my heart.

This was supposed to be a temple built
To You who said the altar would be lit
Forever. And I thought that You had said
A holy altar cannot be a tomb.
(*The Gifts of God*, p. 49)

The poem starts okay. Our house, of course, is our mind. This is Helen saying that my mind belongs to you and come. *I have forgot the glow of diamonds and the glittering of gold that once I thought would lighten up the dark and bring me comfort.* In a sense, what you get is the first part of St. John of the Cross's "nada." In other words, Helen is saying I've given up everything. I have given up diamonds and the glittering of gold. I have given up silver drapes and these wonderfully designed rugs. I have given all this up to make room for you, but you don't come.

And what I'm left with now are *ringless fingers that hold the lamp long since gone out and cold. The wind sings bitterly a chant of fear that echoes round the walls and enters ceaselessly into my heart.* In other words, that there's nothing there. Now I did my part, but you haven't come. So in a sense, this is the dark night without the light. This is the dark night where it seems to be all that there is.

36

Now again there are other poems of Helen's that express something quite, quite different. But what you are getting here are poems written from a place in her that still feels exactly what she is writing. She is not in a sense writing about a state; she's actually writing *from* that state. That's what makes these very, very powerful and sincere. I think it's very hard for students of the Course at some point or another to avoid having this kind of feeling.

You do all the work. And we all know that forgiveness is very difficult and looking at our world differently is very difficult. Looking at abuse and victimization and pain and suffering is very difficult; whether we look at it in ourselves or see it expressed in the world. To feel a sense of peace even in the midst of all that is very hard work. As you work with this but you don't finish, and you're not across the bridge yet; at some point, you are stuck with this.

You know, "I can't go back." In a sense, that's what Helen is saying. I can't go back to all the baubles of the world. I can't go back to the special relationship frame, with the diamonds and the rubies. I can't go back to the silver drapes and the fancy rugs and the diamonds and the glittering of gold, because I've given all that up. But, "You haven't come." Now, of course, what really is being expressed isn't that Jesus hasn't come, but that we haven't gone back yet. We haven't come. We are the ones who wandered away. We are the ones who come back.

What you find in so much of the spiritual literature, certainly in the Christian literature, and in some of Helen's poems, is somehow waiting for Jesus to come. Well, he can't come because he's never left. His love, that thought of love, is in all of us. We're the ones who left. But that's so easily projected just as Helen's poems are expressing, *so easily projected*. As the bride was projecting in *The Spiritual Canticle* of John of the Cross: "Where have you gone? Why can't I see you? Why are you hiding yourself?" When we are the ones who put up the veil, so we can't see.

The blaming of him is an attempt to somehow cover over this searing pain of emptiness. Again, it's beyond pain. The pain is that it's beyond pain. Pain covers over this pain. This is the pain of absolute nothingness. Again this is the wrong-minded "nada." The right-minded "nada" is that there's nothing except God. The wrong-minded "nada" is that there's nothing, period. That's the hopelessness, and that's that despair, and that's when we suddenly feel and believe that our mind that we once thought was holy now is a tomb, and what's being laid to rest in that tomb is our self. That's not a very nice feeling at all.

But the important thing about all this is to recognize that everyone walks this earth with this. This is what it means to be an ego. This is the bottom line of the ego. This is what we cover over. The anger that we feel covers this over. Holding on to our past problems and our past grievances covers this over. Holding on to what we call or think of as our present day problems covers this over. All of our special love objects, our special love addictions, our special love partners cover this over.

Above all, religion covers this over. All religion is an attempt to cover this over. So we make up an imaginary God, write imaginary books about Him, all in an attempt to cover over what the ego is telling us and what's true of everyone who is in this world and in a body. That there is no God; *God is dead; you killed Him*. But that means you're going to die too, and there's nothing. There is no hope. That's the bottom line, and that's what we all attempt to cover over.

Questions

Q: At the time of the new apartment, could Bill receive this as a gift or did Helen realize it?

K: I don't think Helen presented it to him as a gift. It was our secret. I said to Helen I think it would be nice if you wrote

Bill a poem, and that was the end of my nice idea. The next thing I knew, Helen presented me with this because I got the poems first. Bill saw all the poems obviously, but it wasn't connected up with his move. As bad as their relationship was, it would have gotten much, much worse if this was the present.

Q: Which poem was written first?

K: The other poem was written first.

Q: This one seems a lot more angry.

K: Yes, it was a month a part. "The Ancient Love" was written February of 1974. This was written in March, actually two weeks apart. But you can't go by the sequence of poems because remember, the mind isn't linear. It was like Helen would just shift to one part of her mind and you would get a dark night poem. Then in another part, you would get a hopeful poem, love poem. But they were two weeks apart.

Q: I want to go back to talk about the level of despair that we were hearing you read. Is it a one-time deal that someone goes to that place? Or can one experience that many times at that level?

K: I know what the right answer is, right? Or the answer you want to hear? No, I don't think it's a one-time thing. Just like when I talk, usually at greater length, about those six stages in "Development of Trust," I point out that these are not stages you go through and that's it (M-4.I-A). In a sense, they are meant to give an overview of the process, and we're always going through the same stages but in a deeper way. There comes a point when we make the choice once and for all, and that's when we are in the real world. But until then, we go back and forth.

Q: My question is then, if one experiences that enough and gets used to what that's like, is it possible that one could actually let go?

K: Yes, even today. Yes. Yes, absolutely. One of the points of talking about this, and why I'm talking about it is to really point out that this is in everyone. And it's so awful that that could be the motivation for really wanting to get out of this. Now it doesn't mean to die, physically. But it does mean to die to one's ego in the sense of letting it go. As long as you think things are okay, there's no motivation to really change.

That's why it's so important to realize that there are two stages beyond the fourth stage of "Development of Trust." The fourth stage is when things are nice. You know, "this course works." I forgive. I forgave my parents; I forgive this one; I forgive that one. You know, things are okay. I did the Course; I finished. I'm in the real world. There's nothing left. And you missed the last line of that fourth stage. He has not gone as far as he thought (M-4.I-A.6:10).

What poems like this do is to really say, "You know, there's an underside to everything that we do," *even our work with this course*. And it's very easy to use the Course as a defense against really looking at this bleak wasteland that life in the ego is, which is expressed as life here in the body and in the world. And to somehow see that this is more than just living a happier dream here. This is about awakening from the dream. So, yes, there's no question this is something you could choose.

Q: Would you comment on how this would relate to depression, and a clinical diagnosis of what people now call depression. At what point in this process would you say this person is depressed and needs meds or whatever?

K: That's an excellent question. Basically, it's a question of discerning whether you're talking about a depression that, in a sense, is a part of the journey, or what we refer to as a clinical depression. I think that that's extremely important. If you're helping someone, if you are a therapist or you're somehow involved with trying to help guide someone—is the experience something that's more of a psychopathological nature, or is it something that's much more part of a spiritual journey? And there's no easy way to discern that. If you feel that it's a clinical depression then I think you approach it differently. Now ultimately any psychological problem is a defense against one's spirituality, but you have to meet people where they are. And I think it's important to discern when someone is having a breakdown that is really part of the dark night that's going to lead them to the real world, or they are having a breakdown that requires hospitalization. I think there's no easy way. You need people who know what to do, which actually was John of the Cross's point. He talked a lot, a great deal in fact, about how important it was for people who directed other people to really know what they were doing. And I think this is very true.

I remember in the early years, this is one of those god-awful *Course in Miracles'* stories. There was someone who had no psychological training whatsoever, and he took it upon himself because he thought now he was enlightened because of the Course. He probably read it for six months. He thought he really knew everything and so he was now guiding people. He was working with this woman who was very disturbed, and he was telling her it was only the fear of love, and it is okay, we will get through it, etc.

Anyway, he called me up finally and described what the symptoms were, and I said get this woman to a hospital. She's having a psychotic break. This is not a spiritual thing; just get her help. But he didn't know what he was doing. I think someone who knew would have recognized that these were serious psychotic symptoms, and not a spiritual awakening. So I don't have an answer for you specifically, except to say it's very important to discern the difference between, as in this case, clinical depression and what really is like a spiritual dark night. Helen's experiences, for example, were not clinically depressed. They were something much different.

"The Wayside Cross"

Let me read this one. This is called "The Wayside Cross."
This was written two days after the last poem, "Prayer for a
House." It's page 50. Again it's very, very similar in terms of
feeling, "The Wayside Cross."

> I tarry by the wayside. Homeless I
> Return each evening to an empty house
> But to awaken and return each day,
> To wait again in silence and despair.
> How long, O Lord, did You ordain I be
> A dweller in a ghost-house? Shadows come
> And fall across my eyes at night, to bring
> A parody of sleep. By day I go
> In an illusion that I am awake
> To my appointed round of bitterness.
> The cup from which I drink is empty. And
> The crumbs allotted me will not sustain
> My little life but shortly. I retain
> A hope so frail it stifles in the dust
> Of waiting on an ancient way that seems
> To lead to nowhere. I have not forgot
> Your promise. I will wait until You come.
> But I must wait in sorrow, with the song
> Of dying all around me on the road
> On which I stand and wait for Your return.
> How long, O lovely Lord of Life, how long?
> (*The Gifts of God*, p. 50)

That line is taken from one of the Psalms. Again it's the
exact same idea. Helen's mind has become this empty death
house, ghost house, in which there is no hope. And again, it
ends with that same accusation, basically telling Jesus I've
made room for you. Where are you in this? How come you
haven't come back?

"Holy Saturday"

I want to read one more poem. This is the last of the dark night poems. This is "Holy Saturday." There's a little story in back of this too. This is part of a trilogy: "Good Friday," "Holy Saturday," and "Easter." Just for you non-Catholics or non-practicing Christians or non-Christians, in Christianity you have Good Friday when Jesus is crucified. Then he's laid in the tomb, and he's dead. That's Holy Saturday. So Holy Saturday is the worst day. It's bad enough Jesus was killed, but now there's absolutely nothing. That's the despair. And then there's the resurrection on Easter Sunday.

On Easter of that year, April (this is the same year we're talking about 1974), Helen wrote a "Good Friday" poem. It was written for Good Friday. After the poem, I said to her, you know, you should really write an Easter poem. I don't think I said anything about Holy Saturday. Anyway it took many, many months because this was not written until November. Actually the Easter poem was written on November 11 of the same year, but this Holy Saturday poem was written on November 14.

It really seemed obvious after Helen had written it down that she really didn't want to write this poem. This is a very, very bleak poem, probably the bleakest. So again Holy Saturday is that time in the dark night when you only think there's darkness and there is no hope of light.

> The door is solid. Ancient keys are gone.
> The rusted hinge stands firm. The bolt is shut,
> And spiders' castles shimmer in the gleam
> Of tired moonlight. Everything seems put
> In place forever, and decay has come
> To wage a ceaseless war against the hope
> Of sunlight. What was once a window stands
> Like blackness in the dark. My fingers grope
> Along the walls and bleed on granite thorns.

I would not hear You knock. The air is thin,
And whistles through the small remaining gap
Upon the dark that lets the moon's edge in.

I fell so long ago I could not come
To let You enter, even if I heard
You knock against the door. I could not reach
The crumbling handle, nor could speak the word
Of welcome that would ask You enter and
Abide with me. Your light would shock my eyes
Long used to darkness, and to dim effects
That shift like shadows round where someone dies,
And wander back and forth and forth and back
Till light becomes unwanted. Did You say
That You would never leave me till the end?
Time has no meaning now.

Was it a day,
A month, a year, — eternity, — since You
Promised to come? You said You would redeem
The world. Yet I can only see a cross.
The resurrection seems to be a dream.
(*The Gifts of God*, p. 108)

Hopelessness: The Dark Night of the Soul

Again, I think most Course students at some point in their
work with the Course feel that this course will never work for
me. It's the same idea. All I see is a cross. All I see is the ego.
All I see is the profound pain and power of my ego, and I
don't see anything else. And in one sense, that's like an occu-
pational hazard when you work with this course. You do
become in touch with the ego. The Course forces you to do
that. It's not a force in terms of a power. But the Course itself,

in terms of the work you do with it, has as its purpose to get you to look at the ego.

When you look at the ego, the temptation is to see nothing else. That's why it's so important, as I pointed out before, *so important* that you begin to have an experience that there's a loving presence with you that's guiding you through this circle of fear. That there's a light-filled presence guiding you through this darkness; that there's a loving presence guiding you through all this hate. Without that, you just get swallowed into like this morass, this quicksand. And that's what these poems are all expressing.

And that's what John has come through, and that's what he's expressing, in a sense, retrospectively. But in these poems, you're getting it right—in a sense—from the horse's mouth. This was a part of Helen's mind that had never let go of that ego thought system of hopelessness that was there. Her gift to the world is in showing us what the ego thought system is and showing us what the right-minded thought system is, and that there really is a choice.

These poems point out what the real rock bottom, what the culmination of the ego system is; that there's absolute hopelessness. Again, it's beyond the terror; it's beyond the anxiety; it's beyond the pain; it's beyond the hate and the rage and the anger. It's absolute nothingness. It's this bleak, unresponsive death knell. That's all we hear and all we ever experience, and that's what she's saying here. *I have fallen so long ago that even if you came, I would not hear you. I could not reach the crumbling handle nor could speak the word of welcome that would ask you enter and abide with me.* That's how far I have fallen.

Yet it still ends up with that projected image: *But you promised. How long ago was it that you promised and you have not come? How long, O lovely Lord of Life, how long?* It's important, not that everyone feels this kind of devastation, but it's important that you recognize that the entire world, your personal world and the world at large was made to cover this over.

Many of you know the Pulitzer Prize-winning book of Ernest Becker called *The Denial of Death*. I have mentioned it from time to time. His thesis there is that no one wants to deal with death. And then he talks about all the various ways that we defend against death. He says the only thing that works in defending against death, even though it's not true, is religion, because it promises you an afterlife. It promises you something. Becker's point is not that this is true, because he doesn't believe it, but this is what works. This is what people do, because we are trying to deny the hopelessness of death; that death is the ending.

In a sense, that's my point here with these poems. These poems are expressing something that no one wants to have a look at. And yet if we don't look at it in some way, shape, or form, then we will never get past it. It's realizing it's this hopelessness in each of us that will guide us from the ego's point of view as we work with this course. You have to recognize that so you can choose a different guide. Because the temptation is to feel this course may work for other people; it won't work for me.

That's what Helen is telling Jesus in these poems. You don't work for me. You promised you would come, but you haven't come. I gave up everything for you, and now I'm left with absolutely nothing. And that's what people feel with this course. This course has taken all my special relationships away from me and has left me with nothing. Yet I can't go back to the illusions of my past. I can't pay homage to the illusions that the world offers me, but you have given me nothing. That's that awful dark night that precedes the light. But there has to be something in you that has faith. You have faith in someone leading you and faith in the process. This is inevitable, but something, someone will lead you through it.

Questions

I know that there were some hands up before we stopped. Any questions anyone has before we move on? This afternoon will be a little better than this morning, increasingly better than this morning.

Q: Are you referring to two periods of time going through the dark night of the soul? There's the one that causes us to basically search out something like *A Course in Miracles*, and then there's the period of time that you actually get involved in being a student, and there is another part?

K: I think I understand your question.

Q: I'm a pretty young bloke here and the demographic; why is it that students of *A Course in Miracles* are (looking for a very politically correct way to say older)…

K: More mature?

Q: More mature.

K: You asked me two questions. So what do I do now? Now I'm confused. Which one should I answer first and how should I answer them?

Q: The one that brought us here maybe, and the one in the process. Am I correct in saying that there are two dark nights of the soul?

K: The implications of what you are saying, which I think are correct, are that the first dark night of the soul you are talking about is perennial. That's there until we finally choose against it. In fact that was the point I was making reading Helen's poems; that there's an undercurrent of that dark night that's in everyone. Because once you leave home, there's nothing but darkness because home is light.

Then once we start on the process and on the journey of going back, then there are the dark nights. I will discuss that a little bit once I get finished answering questions. The second question was about young people. Basically this isn't a Course for young people. I think that the young people tend to feel that there's hope. They are involved in having families and making money, completing education and having a job and supporting a family and getting a nice car and living in a nice neighborhood and worrying about the schools for their kids, and all the things that normal people do. There's some kind of expectation that the world is going to give you something. It's only when you recognize that the world's not going to give you anything, because the world has nothing to give you that you then look for the other way. Then something like the Course or any other spiritual system would meet that need.

Q: But then there are people that don't think that this is a terrible place. I have friends that think this is a great place. You know, really. They mean it too, and the worst thing they will say is, look, you're going to die someday. Enjoy. This is great while you are here. Just have a good time. So everyone is not aware.

K: Yes, right. That's true. That's true. My point is basically that I think that to be a student of this course, it's important that you feel that nothing here works. That's all. But, yes, there's no question that a lot of people feel this world is great.

The Happy Learner

Let me read you that brief passage that talks about how the Holy Spirit wants us to understand our misery. It's on page 272. It's the beginning of "The Happy Learner" section right at the beginning. It's in the text.

(T-14.II.1:1-3) The Holy Spirit needs a happy learner, in whom His mission can be happily accomplished. You who are steadfastly devoted to misery must first recognize that you are miserable and not happy. The Holy Spirit cannot

teach without this contrast, for you believe that misery *is* happiness.

That's the problem. We believe that it's possible to be happy in this world that's not our home, living in a body that is a travesty of the Self that God created, while alone in this world as an orphan, trying to establish relationships with people who aren't there. Each relationship will ultimately fail in terms of its purpose, which is to bring us happiness and peace, and the whole thing ends in death anyway. There are many, many passages in the Course which reflect this.

The idea that the dark night actually begins when we take the tiny, mad idea of separation seriously, I think is an important one. Because that's the original dark night and that is *the* dark night. When we leave the world of light, we are plunged into darkness, and then we make artificial light. First, there's the ego thought system, which gives us artificial light. And then we make up a world. And then we have a sun, simply talking just about *our* solar system. Then some bright person invents electricity or we have candles and fire. We think this is light; and we think we can see.

All of this, when you analyze it from the Course's point of view, understanding what the ego thought system is, is an attempt to deny the fundamental darkness in which we all live. This is the real suffering. It's an ontological suffering that has never left us, and we desperately try to cover it over.

Again, the value of understanding what the dark night is and certainly understanding the kinds of experiences Helen was reflecting in her poems, not to mention many passages in the Course which reflect that also, is that it helps us realize that Helen is everyone. Helen's ego is everyone's ego. Helen's right mind is everyone's right mind. That's why, while this course was specifically addressed to her and to Bill, it was not their egos that Jesus was exposing. He was exposing everyone's ego because it's the same ego. Everyone again has the same Holy Spirit as their Teacher. Everyone has the same ego that we have to unlearn. And, of course, we all have the same power to choose between them.

Q: This misery that we have to acknowledge, and we talked about our attraction to pain: is it fair to say that the misery and the pain are just sensory responses, which we have taught the body to bring back to us?

K: Absolutely.

Q: It just roots us in the body, and the pain that we feel was the pain that Helen felt in waiting for Jesus to come to her aid; waiting for something outside of her to come to her aid, and that was an expectation of the sensory apparatus of the body to bring her something?

K: That's right. The right-minded view of the body is to see it as the mirror that casts back to us the reflection of what's going on in a mind that we don't know we have. The body really is like a blank slate that simply does what it's told. It sees what the mind wants it to see. It hears what the mind wants it to hear, thinks what the mind wants it to think, and feels what the mind wants it to feel.

Q: The wrong mind?

K: Yes, the wrong mind; but then the right mind also wants us to see things differently.

Q: But the decision maker, what we are in truth, would not feel the pain of the dark night?

K: No, it does feel the pain. When the decision maker listens to the ego, which we all did originally, we feel the pain of that dark night. The ego tells us, yes, we are separated. The separation is real and now you are plunged into darkness. That's what sin and guilt are, and now God's going to punish you, so it's going to be even worse. And this is the reality; this is your reality now. There's that line I always quote from the beginning of Lesson 93: you believe you are "the home of evil, darkness and sin" (W-pI.93.1:1). That's the core belief that everyone who thinks he or she is here believes. That's the dark night. Now, there's no dark night because we are still in the light, so the whole thing is made up. But we all believed it. And then we have to *do* something because it's so painful. Again what's expressed in Helen's poems is really very, very painful. So we cover it over. First we say it's not my fault; it's God's fault. God is the heavy. He is vengeful. He is wrathful. He's going to punish me. He doesn't forgive me. He doesn't come and save me. Then we project the whole thing into a world, live in a body where that thought system in the mind is now buried, but it casts a very ugly and painful shadow in the world.

The end of the text has this line that everyone who wanders in this world is "uncertain, lonely, and in constant fear" (T-31. VIII.7:1). We all wander in this world lonely and in constant fear, but we cover it over. That's the idea. What Jesus does in this course is he lifts the veil, and he says, "Look, this is what's going on."

In his own way, that's what Freud did a hundred years before this. He lifted the veil and said, "Look, there's a cesspool here. This is the problem." We have to look at this. Twenty-five hundred years ago, Plato said the same thing. Look. Wise men throughout history have said look. Because if you don't look, it stays there, and then you defend against it without knowing you are defending against it. Then you live in a world and body, which is not your home, in which you are an orphan. As I said this morning, even if you were led back home, the door would be closed. So there is no hope.

The pain of that is so overwhelming; there's no word strong enough in any language to encompass the pain of that recognition and that experience. So we just cover it over. That's what the body does, and that's what the world does. And that's what all of our special relationships do. But what makes this particularly difficult is that once we do all this, we become the defense. That's the real problem. In other words, we make a world and a body. We make a world to defend against this awesome sense of darkness and bleakness and hopelessness, and then we identify with the body. So the body becomes who we are.

What Is the Body?

There's that one-page summary in Part II of the workbook called "What Is the Body?" which talks about how we identify with the body. We identify with what we believe will make us safe. Let me just look at that with you, page 425 in the workbook. "What Is the Body?"

(W-pII.5:1:1-4) The body is a fence the Son of God imagines he has built, to separate parts of his Self from other parts. It is within this fence he thinks he lives [the word fence, just think of it as a defense. *It is within this fence he thinks he lives*]**, to die as it decays and crumbles. For within this fence he thinks that he is safe from love** [which I will get back to in a minute]**. Identifying with his safety, he regards himself as what his safety is.**

That's a very psychologically acute statement. Identifying with his safety, he regards himself as what his safety is. We make a defense against the mind and the mind choosing love, which is the body. That's the defense—microcosmically. Macrocosmically, it's the whole cosmos, the physical universe. But microcosmically we make the body to keep us mindless, to keep us away from the mind, which has the power to choose against the ego.

Once we make up the body as a defense, we become the body. We regard ourselves as what our safety is. We now think we are the body. That's the problem. Because now that I'm a body and that's my identity and that's my life, so I believe, any thought system that tells me I'm not a body is extinguishing my reality. That's the resistance.

So it's not bad enough that the body is the expression of the pain of this dark night, of this darkness of being outside of our home and never having a way of getting back. Once we become the body, we then experience the pain, which if you think about it makes no sense, which is why the ego never has us think about it. The ego tells us the body will save us from the pain of our annihilation and yet the body is vulnerable to pain, feels pain throughout its whole life, physically and emotionally, and then dies.

In one wonderful passage, Jesus explains all this and says we wanted to ask the ego; but this doesn't make sense. You tell me to make a body in which I will be safe, and then the body dies and I'm not safe in it (T-4.V.4:6)? What the ego does is obliterate the question from awareness. Because I'm not a mind (T-4.V.4:10), I don't even know whom to ask.

It's now a God-given reality, a fact that I'm born into a body. So I have to make the best of what is a miserable situation. That's when people start making fantasies. Religion is just one group of those fantasies: the body is holy; the body is sacred; God created it; and God will reward it with an afterlife.

Or we have economic fantasies or we have political fantasies or social fantasies or romantic fantasies, all kinds of fantasies. This will make me happy. This will work. This will bring me peace. This will bring peace to the planet. This will bring peace to my home. This will give me a lot of money. This will give me a lot of happiness and pleasure. This will give me a longer life. And the whole thing is a massive defense. It's a smokescreen to keep from us the awareness of who we really are within the dream, which is a decision maker that chose the ego and chose wrongly.

And that wrong choice is the cause of the misery, *not the forms in which the misery is expressed*. It's a decision for the ego; that's the suffering. This is not God's ordaining this or Jesus saying you have to suffer or what the churches teach.

Being here is suffering; choosing the ego is suffering. But the problem is what we use to defend against that pain, i.e., the body, becomes our identity. And giving up the body then is experienced by us as painful. Giving up the thought system that made the body is experienced by us as painful. Giving up all our problems, our past history of abuse and victimization is experienced as painful. Even while we think these things are painful, which on one level they certainly are, the pain is that we're attracted to them and don't want to let them go, because we like living in this world. We especially like living in this world when we hate living in this world. Because if you hate living in this world, you believe there's a world.

The ego is very, very clever. How many religions and spiritualities are built around the idea of hating the world and hating the body? The body's bad; sex is bad; having money is bad; enjoying good food is bad; enjoying nature is bad; enjoying friendships is bad. None of this is the problem. The problem is choosing the ego is bad, not bad in a moral sense. It's bad because it doesn't work, and it makes us miserable. It makes us unhappy.

But we think it's the world that makes us this way. We think it's the body that makes us this way. And then we just keep defending against that. We say, okay, I'm in a body. God wants me to suffer to atone for my body's sins. So then you make a religion out of suffering or sacrifice. And it's not the problem. The reason that the journey home is fraught with pain is not because of anything external. It's not because of what religions tell you or the world tells you. It's fraught with pain because there's a part of us that doesn't want to leave. That's the pain.

That's the key thing to understand. There's a part of us that *does not* want to awaken from the dream. To be sure, we want a happier dream, we want a dream where there's less suffering and less pain, less anxiety. We want a dream in which our loved ones are happy, etc. But we don't want to awaken from the dream. That's the problem. That's what the real power of this course is. It exposes that thought. I will read that line again:

(W-pII.5:1:4) Identifying with his safety, he regards himself as what his safety is.

That is who we are. It's not just that the body is my defense. It's now my identity. So I want to bring God into the dream so He will make my body holy. I want to bring Jesus into the dream so he'll make my body holy.

The reason John of the Cross is not the darling of the Catholic Church is no one wants to really understand what he's saying. One of the ways of dismissing him was to make him a saint. He's saying you want to get past this, and the world is not the problem. Everything here is nada. Everything here is nothing.

Where the pain comes from and the suffering comes from is not anything inherent in the body. It's certainly not inherent in God's plan or the Holy Spirit's plan. There really is not a plan anyway. It's inherent in our resistance to awakening from the dream. The last section in Chapter 27 is called "The 'Hero' of the Dream." Hero is in quotation marks because it's not really a hero. The "hero" of the dream is the body. That's the hero of everyone's dream here, collectively and individually.

We all want a happier dream. We don't want to awaken from the dream. We don't want to lose this sense of self. The core of John's experiences was that the lover and the beloved became one. That's what it means to be in the real world. You lose all sense of a separate identity. You get there by realizing everyone here shares the same need, the same interest, the same split mind, which is a reflection of the Oneness of Heaven.

But at the top of the ladder, at the end of the journey, there's no individuality. There is no "I." That's the fear. To rephrase the statement in the text: everyone's afraid they *will be* lifted up and abruptly hurled into reality (T-16.VI.8:1). It doesn't work that way. You go step by step. You go slowly. You go gently. You go kindly. You go in a measured pace that's commensurate with your own level of fear. And what happens is your self gets transformed from a wrong-minded, angry, depressed, guilty self, to a right-minded, forgiving, peaceful and loving self. Only at the very, very end does the whole self disappear. That's at the very end. Until that time comes, you become transformed. You become more right-minded and less wrong-minded.

At the setting out, that seems fine. But as you make your way, it begins to dawn on you where this journey is leading you, and that's when the resistance comes. And with resistance comes pain and suffering. When you are driving in your car and your foot's on the accelerator and the emergency brake is on, your tires suffer. Your engine suffers. The problem is not inherent in the tires or the engine. Something is wrong with how you are driving; namely, you have the brake on. As we make our way on our journey home, being right-minded and following Jesus and learning to forgive, there's still another part of us that has our foot on the brake. And after a while that becomes painful, because you keep pressing forward on the gas, and you don't go. And then you start smelling burning rubber and you know there's something wrong. And then your engine tells you there's something wrong.

I remember once I had a good friend who had rented a car and had a house upstate New York. And she lived in New York and she drove this rented car upstate. And the whole way up, she had the car in second, and she destroyed the engine. The problem was not the car. That's what we are all doing. That's where the pain comes from. That's where the conflict comes from.

So it's important to identify the problem. If you don't identify the problem, you can't do anything about it. You may ask Jesus for help until you are blue in the face. You won't get the answer because you're asking him the wrong question. You will get the answer you want to your question, but it won't get you home. You have to ask him the right question.

What Jesus does in this course is train us to ask him the right question. Help me look at my brother through the eyes of peace and not through the eyes of judgment, as he told Helen once. That's the right question. Please help me look at this brother through the eyes of peace, not the eyes of judgment; not Jesus tell me what to say; not Jesus tell me what to do. Help me look at this person the way you do. Help me look at the world through your eyes instead of my eyes.

Then there won't be any suffering. There won't be any pain. Then there will be only peace until you get frightened. And when you get frightened, then you put on the brake even as your foot is on the accelerator. And then you will experience conflict. Conflict is another way of expressing pain. Resistance is conflict. Conflict is resistance and that's where the pain comes from.

Questions

Q: You probably answered this question about three times already. I'm into this thing also with the despair. There have been so many times when I get up, I will just be in that space, and I know there is an "I" who is in the space. I'm beginning to think that judgment seems to be the issue here; if I didn't judge the despair as despair, or if I didn't do anything with it, I would get used to this enough that pretty much it would be a natural progression of things to just kind of dissipate on their own.

K: Right.

Q: That which is judging is me, trying to protect this?

K: In "The Rules for Decision" that begins Chapter 30, under the first rule for decision there's this line that's in italics, which means it's emphasized, *do not fight yourself,* which in other words is saying do not judge yourself (T-30.I.1:7). Once you judge against the ego, once you fight against the ego, once you want to change the ego, you are giving it a reality it doesn't have.

That's why nothing ever changes in this world. No revolution really works long term because you don't change anything. You change externals. You don't change the thought system. If you don't change the thought system, nothing will change. But the way you change the thought system is to expose it for the nothingness it is.

If you fight against it, if you want to change it; whether it's an external expression of it or the internal thought system, nothing will happen. The most fundamental definition of forgiveness comes in the workbook that says forgiveness is still, and quietly does nothing. It merely looks, and waits, and judges not (W-pII.1.4:1,3). It looks. It waits because it is patient, and it doesn't judge. That's the definition. That's the operational definition of forgiveness. You don't change. You don't change someone else. You don't change yourself. And when you let your ego go by looking at it for what it is, for the nothingness it is, the love, which the ego was concealing, would automatically flow through you. And you will do and say whatever will be loving.

Q: So stop interpreting anything.

K: Yes, don't analyze. There's a line in the Course that says analysis is of the ego. Don't analyze. In fact, what it actually says is the ego analyzes; the Holy Spirit accepts (T-11.V.13:1).

Q: In the heat of what happens one is not cognizant enough to know that interpretation as…

K: What you are doing?

Q: But after you have done it enough, you go "I got it."

K: Right. You are right. That's right. You may be stupid but you aren't stupid. Afterward, I say you know, something is not working here. Don't analyze your ego. Don't analyze this course. Just learn how to recognize the symptoms of your choosing the ego. You get angry. You get depressed. You get guilty. You get mildly annoyed. You find yourself criticizing. You find yourself fantasizing about things. Whatever it is that's not an expression of absolute and certain peace is of the ego.

And all you have to know is I've chosen the ego again. Why? Because I'm trying to protect *my self.* I'm trying to preserve this identity because the ego has told me if I forgive, if I don't judge, I will disappear, which isn't true. What will happen if I forgive and I don't judge is I will be happier. I will still have the same identity. I will still wear the same clothes. I will still see the same image in the mirror every morning. But I will be happier. I will be less angry. I will be less guilty. I will be more peaceful. I will be more loving. I will be more caring. I will see shared interests instead of separate interests. That's what will happen.

Again, it's only at the very end of the journey that we disappear with Jesus into the presence beyond the veil, as he says (T-19.IV-D.19:1). That's at the very, very end. You don't have to worry about that. Because by the time that comes, you won't have a self that you're identifying with, so it will just fall away. But it won't be taken away from you. Your self will be transformed step-by-step as you make your way home.

There won't be any suffering until you get frightened. And like the gospel story of Peter who walks on water, and all of a sudden he says, "Oh my God, I'm walking on water," and goes plop. Oh my God, I'm being loving and peaceful. I'm not angry anymore. I'm not carrying around a grievance of forty years. Then you get frightened and then you go running back to your friends, as the Course says, and your friends are sin, guilt, fear, and death (T-19.IV-D.6:2-3).

Q: The mind witnesses the death of the body. The pain continues because it's in the mind?

K: Right.

Q: It keeps witnessing the deaths of bodies, because I'm sure that it then decides to select another body identification. But what is the rationale?

K: You mean why do we keep coming back?

Q: Yes.

K: In one sense, the ego would say, "You know, we really screwed up last time. This time it will be different." Or it could say, "You know, the last time was pretty miserable but this current lifetime is really worse and you are such an abused victim. This is wonderful. You know, God will really forgive you this time because of all the abuse. After this lifetime, which will be really awful, you will have completed your atonement." *The ego's atonement!*

Q: It never really questions the fact that the pain continues? It's ongoing.

K: Remember, you are talking about the ego. If what you are really asking is doesn't the decision maker recognize that coming back and back and back is just more and more pain? The answer is not as long as the decision maker identifies with the ego, which you do while you are here in a body, or think you are here in a body, or when you are not in a body. It doesn't matter since no one is here in a body anyway. Remember the decision maker is outside of time and space where everything has already happened simultaneously.

All the incarnations have occurred at the same time. As long as you stay with the ego, you just keep replaying the same stuff over and over again. The more suffering, the better; the more abuse, the better; the more victimization, the better because you can point the accusing finger and say you are the one who did it, not me. And God will seem to punish you. Until the time comes outside of time and space when the decision maker says there has to be another way. Then you start listening to the Holy Spirit Who gives you different advice.

Q: You said that we created the body to get away from the mind. Correct?

K: Yes. Yes. The Course would say miscreate the body.

Q: Miscreate? Okay. But that was to get away from the right mind?

K: Strictly speaking, to get away from the decision-making mind, because the decision maker has the power to choose the ego or choose against the ego. The part of us that likes being an ego, likes being separated, doesn't want to have that decision changed. One of the best ways not to change your mind is to not know you have a mind. If I don't know I have a mind, how could I change it?

Q: Okay, but the mind we think we have is the wrong mind.

K: Yes, because once we choose the wrong mind, we forget we have a right mind.

Q: When the Course talks about corrected perception, and that we get a little bit closer and a little bit closer, does that corrected perception lead us back to the decision maker?

K: Absolutely, yes.

Q: It is kind of a natural progression that the decision maker is the Holy Spirit?

K: No.

Q: Okay. Help me see the difference between the decision maker and the Holy Spirit.

"Mind 101"

K: Let me give a quick class in Mind 101. The split mind has two thought systems in it. It has the thought system of the ego that believes separation is real and is good, and then is sinful. And there's the Holy Spirit's thought system, which is the Atonement, which says the separation never happened. When the idea of being separate from God first arose—what the Course refers to as the tiny, mad idea—both of those thought systems arose with it, which are really two different ways of looking at the tiny, mad idea of being separate from God.

One says the separation is real. The other says there is no separation. Then there's also a third part of the mind that chooses between one of those two. The ego is nothing more or less than a response to the tiny, mad idea that says, yes, it's real. The Holy Spirit is nothing more or less than a response to the tiny, mad idea that says it's not real. And the decision maker is the part of the mind that chooses which to identify with.

We choose the ego because we like the idea of being separated, like the idea of being an individual, like the idea of having a separate consciousness, a differentiated self. Once we do that, for all intents and purposes, the right mind disappears. It doesn't really disappear but it's buried, because we've now identified with the ego. The fear we then have, because we like being an ego, is what if the part of my mind that chose the ego decides to change its mind and choose the Holy Spirit instead? If that happened, my separated, individual self would disappear. Because the only thing that keeps my self intact and alive and existing is my belief in it. If I withdraw my belief in it, it will disappear because it's inherently nothing.

Then the part of me that likes being me, that likes being an ego, has to come up with a way, a strategy, to ensure that I never change my mind. Because if at some point I go back to that decision maker and I recognize what I chose, and how badly I chose it, I will change my mind. At which point the ego, as the Course says, disappears back into the nothingness from which it came (M-13.1:2).

Therefore, to ensure that I never change my mind, I make myself mindless. If I don't know I have a mind, I can't change it. Well, how do I make myself mindless? I project my self out of the mind, make up a world and make up an individual self in a body. Once I'm in a body, I forget where I came from. All that I know is that I exist. As I grow up, I learn I'm the product of a sperm and an egg, nothing to do with the mind. That's the ego strategy. That's what this entire world witnesses to: the brilliance of that strategy. It's ingenious. Everyone here walks around in a perpetual mindless state, and we think all of our problems are external.

There's that very important line that says of all the many causes of your suffering, never once did you think your guilt was among them (T-27.VII.7:4). We are very good as societies and as individuals in identifying the causes of suffering. We are very sophisticated, very brilliant and we are all wrong. The cause of my suffering is my decision for the ego, my decision for guilt.

But how do I know that? How can I change that when I don't know I have a mind? I'm mindless. Therefore, I need a thought system and I need a teacher of that thought system to instruct me that what I'm seeing externally in my relationship with you is a projection. Let's say that my relationship with you is not good, and that there's a lot of anger and hurt. I'm taught that what's going on between you and me is a projection, "the outside picture of an inward condition" (T-21.in. 1:5), of a decision my mind made to be separated, to be with my ego.

And I learn step by step to see everything that's perceived externally is a projection of a decision my mind made. That's how I begin the process of learning I have a mind. So that one could very nicely summarize *A Course in Miracles*, by saying it's a journey from mindlessness to mindfulness. Jesus begins where we think we are, which is in the body in the world, and leads us back from the body to the mind. So we become mindful instead of mindless and we can choose again. Which is why, the very end of the text, the very last section, is called "Choose Once Again" (T-31.VIII).

Q: Would you like to comment on the Holy Spirit helping out on the journey to the corrected perception?

K: The way the Holy Spirit gets us back is when we come to Him for help and say, "Blah, blah, blah, blah." This is blah, blah, blah—all the time—and the poor guy has an earache. What He says is, "Calm down. The world you see is an outward picture of an inward condition. You are never upset for the reason you think (W-pI.5). What you're seeing outside again is a projection of what you're seeing inside." He gently, calmly, lovingly leads us back from the world to the mind. That's how He helps us.

That is until I get fearful of my mind; again, because the ego tells me God will destroy me if He ever finds me in my mind. When I get fearful, I get resistant to this course and resistant to forgiveness and resistant to the Holy Spirit. I kick them away again. I choose the ego again. And then I'm off and running, until the pain starts building up and the misery starts and the unhappiness comes and I say, "Oh, there's something wrong here. Oh right, that's what is wrong. I forgot to ask for help."

Question: Resistance

Q: When I do my workbook lessons, and I just don't have time to do as many as the Course says, is that choosing with the ego?

K: That's resistance. If this course were the most important thing in your life, because returning home and awakening from the dream was the most important thing in your life, I assure you, you would have lots of time. You would remember God not only ten times every hour, thirty times every hour, if that were the most important thing.

So what are the real benefits of the workbook? In fact, I think the *greatest* benefit of the workbook is to have us realize how much we don't want to do the workbook. How much we don't want to return home and awaken from the dream, and then helping us to forgive ourselves for not wanting to return home. That's what resistance is. That's the real value of the workbook; not that you judge yourself when you forget the lesson. Not that you buy an alarm clock or an alarm wristwatch that will go off every twelve minutes to remind you to think of God or the lesson, which misses the whole point. Rather forget, as everyone will forget. Let the world intrude once again. As soon as you become aware of it, recognize this is what I did right at the beginning. I believed the ego was more valuable than God. I believed special love was more valuable than God's Love. I believed time was more valuable to me than eternity. I believed my important work here and my important relationships here were more important to me than my relationship with God and my function in Heaven of creating.

I'm just doing it again. By forgetting to think of the lesson every hour, I'm doing microcosmically what we all did macrocosmically, except now I know that's what I'm doing. And so by forgiving myself for not doing the lesson perfectly, I'm forgiving myself for having made an imperfect choice. Without judgment, without guilt, simply saying that's what I did, not because I'm sinful but because I'm afraid of love. I mean, who in his right mind wouldn't do the workbook perfectly, if you knew that was going to give you what you want? The problem is we aren't so sure we want it.

The problem with *Course in Miracles'* students, just to stay with that particular perverse group, is that they're so arrogant that they think they love this course. If you loved this course, you wouldn't need it. If you loved this course and where it's leading you, you wouldn't need it because you would already be there. So the fact that you need this course is telling you that you don't love it, and you don't love its teacher, because look what a mockery the world has made of him. That's very helpful information to have. That's what speeds you along the journey. You don't have to agonize. You don't have to force anything on yourself. You don't have to try to fool Jesus. The idea that you have to do the workbook perfectly is coming from this crazy idea that Jesus is up in Heaven with a scorecard judging you. Just as the Bible implies, he's going to come back on clouds of glory with a big notebook, judging all the good guys and the bad guys, which means he must be paying attention. How else would he know who are the sheep and who are the goats? Which is the wheat and which is the chaff? How would he know if he weren't observing you and keeping notes? He's over sixty. His memory isn't that good so he has to keep notes. [Laughter]

But that's the insanity people have. It's subtle. What I said may sound crazy, but that's what people must believe. Why else would you agonize over doing the workbook perfectly? It's so much better to do it imperfectly, which comes perfectly natural in this unnatural world, and once again then forgiving yourself for it. It's much kinder. It's more loving. It's gentle. It's soft. It's easy. There's no judgment involved. That's how the Holy Spirit helps us.

Light in the Dream

What I wanted to talk about, which I have already been talking about, is our resistance to returning home to the light. Again, it's really just hinted at in John's poems because he's writing after the fact. He does elaborate on this when he's writing his commentary. But it's very clear in Helen's poems, at least in terms of the effects.

I want to read you one passage from the text. It's page 378, which is one among several references that make it very clear what happens when we choose the light. It's the section called "Light in the Dream." It's actually a particularly beautiful section but I'm not going to read the beautiful part. This is at the beginning.

(T-18.III.1:1) You who have spent your life in bringing truth to illusion, reality to fantasy, have walked the way of dreams.

Now the Course process is the opposite. We are supposed to bring the illusion to the truth. An example of bringing truth to illusion is when you believe Jesus or the Holy Spirit or God are involved in the world. That's the example of bringing truth to the illusion. That was the big and tragic mistake that the earlier followers of Jesus, whoever they were, made because they brought him into the dream.

His whole message was come to where I am. Instead the world brought him to where they were and then built idols instead: what in the clarification of terms is referred to as the "bitter idols" (C-5.5:7). We always want to bring truth into the dream to make the dream better, instead of bringing the dream to the reality.

(T-18.III.1:2-5) For you have gone from waking to sleeping, and on and on to a yet deeper sleep. Each dream has led to other dreams, and every fantasy that seemed to bring a light into the darkness but made the darkness deeper. Your goal was darkness, in which no ray of light could enter. And you sought a blackness so complete that you could hide from truth forever, in complete insanity.

What Jesus is talking about here is that once we chose to leave the light and went into the ego's darkness, we became the darkness. And so our goal was darkness in which no ray of light could ever enter. The ray of light is when the decision maker chooses the Holy Spirit as its Teacher. That's the ray of light.

I think the best way to understand the phenomenon of Jesus is that when he appeared in the world, the decision makers in the mind, in the Sonship, chose the thought of light, chose the thought of love, which is abstract, non-specific, because it's in the mind. That then became reflected in the dream, as this shining, resplendent figure of light and love that appeared. And of course he's not the only one throughout history who has appeared. The person that the world identified as Jesus, by whatever name he was called, is not the light. He's a fragment of the light. He's a symbol of the light. He's a reflection of the light. He's not the light. The light is the thought of love that is in everyone's mind.

What did the world do? It worshipped the symbol. And it made the symbol into an idol, which is the Course's word for special love objects. It enshrined him in stone as a thing, as a body, as a concept, as a theology. It wrote a book about him and stamped the book "holy." It built religions around him and stamped them as "holy," missing the whole point. He was not the light.

He was a reflection of the light that we all in our minds chose as a thought. And we are that light as well. Jesus is just a symbol. As he says in the teacher's manual, the name of Jesus Christ is but a symbol (M-23.4:1). It's a symbol for a love that is not of this world, but it is of the right mind that we all share. But our goal was darkness so we brought the light into the darkness.

(T-18.III.1:3) Each dream has led to other dreams, and every fantasy that seemed to bring a light into the darkness [such as the birth of Jesus coming into the world as the gospel myths tell us] **but made the darkness deeper.**

Because it made the world real; it made the body real. It made the thought of sin real because what is the core of the myth? God sent His only Son into the world to forgive sin. Now why would God do that unless he believed sin were real? And why would God do that unless He were insane? There is no sin. There is no world. So how could God send His Son into a world that doesn't exist to redeem it from a sin that never happened? That's what this is talking about.

But that's what we all do when we ask Jesus for help here, instead of asking his help that we come to where he is in the mind so we could make the same choice that he made. We could be the same thought of love that he is, not as a body. Why do you want to identify with a body? You want to identify with a thought, and he represents the thought of who we are. As long as we think we are a body, we need a symbol that is a body that is a right-minded symbol. We are the wrong-minded symbols of the body.

He is a right-minded symbol. And again he's not the only symbol. We need a right-minded symbol to correct the wrong-minded symbol. When we do that, the wrong and right-minded symbols disappear, and all that's left is what is beyond the symbol. That's the love that John was talking about in his poems.

(T-18.III.1:5-8) And you sought a blackness so complete that you could hide from truth forever, in complete insanity. What you forgot was simply that God cannot destroy Himself [and we are part of God]. **The light is *in* you. Darkness can cover it, but cannot put it out.**

Now that's what Jesus' message was two thousand years ago. The light is in you. It's in your mind. The resplendence you see in me, he would say, is simply a reflection of the resplendence in you. And the darkness of the world, the thought system of the ego, can't put it out.

But then, this is what happens:

(T-18.III.2:1) As the light comes nearer [which means as we choose the light because the light doesn't move. As the light comes nearer, as we go back to the light] **you will rush to darkness, shrinking from the truth, sometimes retreating to the lesser forms of fear, and sometimes to stark terror.**

That's resistance. That's resistance to the light. That's when, as John said in "The Living Flame," that we had experienced the love as being oppressive. At the point that he's writing from, it's now consummate but it had been oppressive. "A living flame of love that tenderly wounds my soul in its deeper center since now you are not oppressive."

This passage I just read to you is saying the love is still oppressive. The light is still oppressive. It's threatening. At the same time I'm going towards the light with my foot on the accelerator, my other foot is on the brake and my hand is on the emergency brake. This is everyone's experience. There are earlier sections which make the same point. Jesus says when you take my hand on the journey, your ego will become retaliative (T-8.V.5:6). When you begin to take the Holy Spirit's evaluation of you, instead of the ego's evaluation of you, your ego will become vicious. That's resistance. That's our fear of the love that is our true self that would awaken us from this dream.

What's very, very helpful is to be aware of how much you don't want to leave the dream. Otherwise you will do one of two things. You will come down very hard on yourself when you find yourself choosing the ego again and accuse yourself of being a *Course in Miracles'* failure. Or, you will pretend that you really love this course, and you're really one step away from the real world, if not already in the real world. And then you will start hearing and telling everyone what you are hearing, how the Holy Spirit is telling you to do this, that, and the other thing, and what the Holy Spirit tells you to tell other people, and on and on and on.

Because you brought the light to the darkness, and then it gets enveloped in the darkness of specificity, but you don't know you have done it. That explains why for two thousand years otherwise well-meaning Christians can attack other people in the name of Jesus. I mean it makes absolutely no sense. To a sane, rational mind, it's insane that you could have crusades, inquisitions, persecutions, and launch wars in the name of the Prince of Peace. It makes no sense unless you understand psychology, which explains how when you are repressing something, you will never know that you are projecting it, because you don't know you repressed it.

You think what you are projecting is real. What you are repressing is the belief that you are the guilty sinner. You are the home of evil, darkness, and sin because you're the one who separated from the Love of God, and you're the one who crucified Christ by separating from the Oneness of Heaven. And rather than look at that you project it outside, and you see sinners and heathens and pagans all around you that you have to attack and crucify and persecute and kill because God told you to.

Well that's true, god did tell you; but it was the ego's god that told you. Again, none of this makes any sense to a rational mind, but no one here is rational. Because people here believe in the height of irrationality; namely, that part of God could separate from Him and that God can destroy Himself. Once you accept that basic insanity, every other thought you have is insane.

All your thoughts about God are then insane, or your thoughts about Jesus or any other messenger of Heaven is insane. And all your thoughts about *A Course in Miracles* will be insane too, because you will totally misunderstand it. Because it's not about bringing the light into darkness; it's about bringing the darkness of the ego to the light of truth. But again you must be aware of your fear because you have identified with the thought of darkness. You have identified with the body of darkness thinking it's the light.

From Darkness to Light

I want to look at another section with you. It's in the text, page 199. It's the section "From Darkness to Light," and we will start with paragraph 3.

(T-11.III.3:1-5) O my child, if you knew what God wills for you, your joy would be complete! And what He wills has happened, for it was always true. When the light comes and you have said, "God's Will is mine," you will see

such beauty that you will know it is not of you. Out of your joy you will create beauty in His Name, for your joy could no more be contained than His. [Now this next sentence is the problem.] **The bleak little world will vanish into nothingness, and your heart will be so filled with joy that it will leap into Heaven, and into the Presence of God.**

Now what's wrong with that sentence? What's wrong with that sentence is that that's the end of me. The bleak little world is our world, both cosmically in terms of the world at large as well as microcosmically, the world of our personal world. The bleak little world will vanish into nothingness, because such it always was and such it will always be. Nothing outside of God can be anything, except nothing.

...and your heart will be so filled with joy that it will leap into Heaven, and into the Presence of God.

That's the yearning. That's what pulls us. At the same time, that's what frightens us. So again, in John's poems you don't get the resistance. It's hinted at in terms of the past, but you don't get it in terms of the present because he already is beyond it. Remember how in "The Dark Night" he talks about one "dark night fired with love's urgent longings." That's what impels us forward because in everyone's mind is that memory of Who we really are as part of love. And that's what pulls us and that's what this is expressing.

...your heart will be so filled with joy that it will leap into Heaven, and into the Presence of God.

And yet there's the part of us that is identified with our bodies, identified with our psychological, physical selves that has identified with this world as our home. As awful as it may be, it is still our home. That's the part that resists leaping into our Father's Arms. That's the fear. And basically the ego's fear is not of that, because it doesn't know about love. Its fear is that the decision maker would choose against it, would choose against the ego and for love, which is the end of the ego. And the part of us that identifies with the ego thought system, that's the part that becomes bitterly afraid.

What Helen's poems don't say, is as painful as the experiences are that the poems reflect, that that is what she secretly wants, which is what we all secretly want. We all want to experience the bleakness of that nothingness, of that darkness, of that cosmic darkness, and not be responsible for it. Because in Helen's poems, Jesus is the one who hasn't shown up. Just as in John's *Spiritual Canticle* at one point, the bride complains to the bridegroom, as I've been saying, "Where are you? Why are you hidden from me?"

I have quoted often, today, as well, the line that the world you see is an outward picture of an inward condition. There's a parallel line that takes that thought and extends it one step further. It says a few chapters later: perception is an outside picture of an inward condition—a secret wish, an image that you want to be true (T-24.VII.8:8-10). The world we perceive, the world we experience is an outward picture of a secret wish, an image that we want to be true.

What is that wish and what is that image? It's the wish to be separated, to be a creature of darkness *but* not to be held accountable for it. That's the image that we want to be true, what later on in the text is referred to as the face of innocence (T-31.V.4:1). I think that is without question the most difficult part of this course, not only to understand but to accept as true for us. Our secret wish, the image we want to be true is that we be separate, but it not be our fault.

My image is I'm a separated self but someone else did it to me. Someone else made me this way. And the way our individual dreams begin as bodies is clearly someone made us this way. A sperm and an egg united, and we are the effect. We have nothing to do with this. It's not our fault. We did not choose the genetic structure of the sperm and the egg. We did not choose how the chromosomes inter-reacted; which are the recessive genes; which are the dominant genes.

It's tailor-made. The world we live in, the world we are born into is tailor-made to fulfill that secret wish of the ego: the image that we want to be true. I exist as a separate self but it is not my fault. It is not my responsibility. I am innocent. I'm innocent of my gender. I'm innocent of my race. I'm innocent of my socio-economic status. I'm innocent of the color of my hair, the size of my nose, the color of my eyes, my brain capacity. I'm innocent of everything. It's that damn sperm and that damn egg. I had nothing to do with it. Perfect!

Since we are taught in this course that purpose is everything, this serves a mighty purpose from the ego's point of view. We keep our separate identity but we can't be held accountable for it. Someone else is responsible.

Behind Helen's poems is that secret wish. I want to feel abandoned. I want to feel betrayed. I want to feel the promises to me have been broken and not kept. I want to feel that my house is now empty and bleak. I want to feel all the evocative things that she describes in those poems. That's the truth. That's the only truth within this dream. It's our dream. *That's the truth.* That is the bad news on the one hand because of what it means. But the good news is that if it is my dream, I can change it.

That's the good news of this course: it's my dream. It's my dream of being unfairly treated. I can change how I feel. Within my life, I can't change what people do to me, but I can change how I look at what people do to me: *how I look at it.* In that line: "Beware of the temptation to perceive yourself unfairly treated" (T-26,X,4;1), we see the whole Course summarized in terms of what forgiveness means. We are all tempted to perceive ourselves unfairly treated. That's the heart of all four of Helen's poems. I've been unfairly treated. You lied to me Lord, how long, how long are you going to stay away from me?

Well, the truth of the matter is she is staying away from him. We are staying away from him because that's what keeps our individual self intact. That's the source of our guilt.

74

Not that we did it eons and eons and eons ago. There are no eons and eons ago. We are doing it right now. As Helen was taking the Course down, Bill asked the question (basically it's the fundamental ego question), "How could this have happened?" And the answer, which is incorporated now in Chapter 4, is why do you ask why something happened long ago when you're still choosing it now (T-4.II. 1:1-3)? It's a very practical answer, but it's the answer that is true for all of us.

We are all choosing now to stay away from love. Because in the presence of love we will disappear; the world will vanish into nothingness, and we will leap into Heaven into the presence of God. In the presence of God, there is no individuality. There is no uniqueness; there is no differentiation; there is no consciousness. There is nothing but perfect Love, which is who we are. That's the fear. And we project our guilt wildly and madly all around us; and we attack and blame everyone and everything.

And then Jesus says, which I mentioned earlier, a line like this:

(T-11.III.3:6) I cannot tell you what this will be like, for your heart is not ready.

Just as John could not explain the last wonderful stanza of "The Living Flame of Love" except for one paragraph, and he's never at a loss for words; he writes and writes and writes. But there he says; there's nothing I could say about this.

(T-11.III.3:7) Yet I can tell you [Jesus goes on], and remind you often, that what God wills for Himself He wills for you, and what He wills for you is yours.

That he can tell us, and that's what he tells us in this course. In other words, everything else is made up because nothing here is God's Will. God's Will is perfect Love and perfect peace and perfect Oneness. Nothing here is that.

(T-11.III.4:1-3) The way is not hard, but it *is* very different. Yours is the way of pain, of which God knows nothing. That way is hard indeed, and very lonely.

Jesus says my way is not hard. All you have to do is accept what I say is the truth and look at the ego and not take it seriously. What could be hard about that? But if you are wedded to pain, if you are wedded to remaining in this dream, if you are wedded to this separated self that you want to accept no responsibility for, then it is very hard and very lonely.

(T-11.III.4:4) Fear and grief are your guests, and they go with you and abide with you on the way.

That's how we all live. That's how we all wander in this world, but we blame everyone and everyone else for it. And even if you blame yourself, the self you are blaming is still the product of your parents and your environment. When you blame yourself, you're not blaming your mind. You are blaming your physical, psychological self, which is the effect of what was done to you or what was failed to be done to you or for you. The ego doesn't care whether it projects guilt onto your body, your parents' body, or anyone else's body as long as it's away from the mind. And since we are mindless creatures, which is what it means to be in a body, there's no way we can change our minds.

(T-11.III.4:5) But the dark journey is not the way of God's Son.

Jesus is saying mine is not the way of pain. Mine is not the way of suffering. However, when you resist me, that's where the pain and suffering come from. I want to help you realize that the pain and suffering you experience comes from your rejecting me and my help—not from whatever you attribute it to. Because when you reject me and my help, you will feel guilty because your rejecting me is reminiscent of your original rejection of God, which is the birthplace of guilt.

That's what he was always telling Helen personally, and that's what he is telling her in this course, as well as everyone else. Your pain and suffering and misery are not coming because of anything here. It has nothing to do with me. It has nothing to do with God. There's nothing holy or sacred or redemptive about it. Your pain and suffering come when you choose against love. And since I am the symbol of love for you, it happens when you choose against me. But the dark journey is not the way of God's Son.

(T-11.III.4:6-8) Walk in light and do not see the dark companions [the dark companions are not the devils or Satans or the demons. The dark companions are fear and grief and guilt and suffering. Walk in light and do not see the dark companions], **for they are not fit companions for the Son of God, who was created *of* light and *in* light. The Great Light always surrounds you and shines out from you. How can you see the dark companions in a light such as this?**

But if the dark companions are my friends and the dark companions are what keep me being me, then I will hold on to them. Because I don't want to see the light; because in the light, my dark companions don't exist. Darkness is not an ontological state. It's the absence of light. Or even better, it's the *belief* in the absence of light because light doesn't go anywhere. But if I am the absence of light, if I am a creature of darkness and guilt, fear and grief, and pain are my allies, if not my very self, then I will be afraid of the light.

I read earlier, as I go towards the light, I will go back into darkness. Fifteen hundred years ago, St. Augustine, who knew about darkness, said: why is it that when I start going to the light, I'm thrown back into the darkness? And he knew about guilt. Because we are afraid of being without the guilt; we are afraid of being without the fear. That's what's important to understand. What this course brings to contemporary spirituality is understanding how attracted we are to guilt, pain, and death—how attracted we are to remaining in this dream.

That's why words like this, which are so clear and unequivocal—you may quibble about a sentence here and there that you don't understand and what does this "it" refer to—but you can't dismiss over and over again these clear, clear statements of what this course is saying. Why is it we don't see it? Why is it we don't understand it? And why is it that we do not live it? It's not because we are bad. It's not because we are stupid. It's because we are terrified. This explains why we are terrified.

It's very important to understand that so you do not beat up on yourself. It will also help you to be kinder towards other people who are doing the very same thing you are. Everyone in this world is lonely and afraid. We are told early in the text that frightened people can be vicious (T-3.I.4:2). Jesus is not denying that there are vicious things that go on in this world. Merciless, cruel, awful things go on that people do. But they do it because they're afraid, not because they are evil or wicked or sinful.

I think the hardest thing to practice in this course is the principle that you either forgive everyone or you forgive no one. There's a line that says you reach Heaven together or not at all (T-19.IV-D.12:7-8). If you exclude one member of the Sonship, you have destroyed the Sonship and crucified Christ again, because the definition of Christ is His perfect wholeness. Remember, Christ has nothing to do with Jesus.

The definition of Christ in this course is His perfect wholeness. Take one part of Christ out, one part of the Sonship out and label it sinful and deserving of your judgment, and you've destroyed the wholeness of Christ because that's what Christ is, is wholeness. That's what makes this course so difficult. Forgiveness is for all, or else it's for no one.

I always love to quote the beginning of Helen's poem, "The Gifts of Christmas," because it's such a wonderful example of this. It starts out "Christ passes no one by. By this you know He is God's Son" (*The Gifts of God*, p. 95). *Christ passes no one by.* That's how you know He is God's Son. Think of those lines or any of the other lines in the Course that say the same thing whenever you are tempted to exclude someone: someone on the news that you don't like, someone in your office, a seeming friend or someone in your family or someone sitting in this room. Whenever you are tempted to judge someone, thereby excluding him or her from the Sonship, think of that line. *Christ passes no one by. By this you know He is God's Son.*

So if you seek to exclude someone, it's because you want to exclude everyone, including yourself and including Jesus who you may profess to love. You can't love him if you don't love everyone, because everyone has that same image of love *that Jesus is*—without exception. The worst villain in history, the worst villain in your life, has that same expression, that same thought of love in them as Jesus does, and as everyone else does. If you don't allow everyone back into the Sonship, you are allowing no one back in, including yourself and including Jesus. And are you willing to make that statement?

That's what will help you when you are tempted to justify and rationalize your anger. You know, this course never says don't get angry. It says don't justify your anger. There's a big, big difference. When you find yourself getting angry and picking a fight with someone, don't come down hard on yourself. Simply say I'm doing it again. I must be afraid of love because love is all-inclusive, and I'm afraid of walking in the light. Because I can't walk in the light if I exclude anyone, which actually is how this section ends. Again:

(T-11.III.4:8-9) How can you see the dark companions in a light such as this? If you see them, it is only because you are denying the light.

Since purpose is everything, why do I deny the light? Why would anyone deny the light? It's the only thing that will make us happy. We deny the light because our bodies, our physical, separated selves cannot exist in the light. And then Jesus asks us:

(T-11.III.4:10) But deny them instead [deny the dark companions instead], **for the light is here and the way is clear.**

The way we deny the dark companions is to look at them, not judge them, and say I have chosen them because I'm afraid; not because I'm evil, not because I'm sinful. Everyone has chosen them, not because they are bad or evil or wicked, but because they're afraid too. And guess what? Everyone is afraid. The core experience of Christ's vision (in one sense that's the goal of the Course to have us attain this) is to realize that everyone in this world is the same. Everyone has the same wrong mind: a thought system of hate, murder, pain, and death. Everyone has the same right mind: a thought system of Atonement and forgiveness and peace and healing. And everyone has the same decision-making power. *Everyone.*

That's Christ's vision. No one is excluded from that. What you ask for help with, once again, is you ask Jesus to help you look at someone the way he sees them, and then forgive yourself when you don't ask him. The reason you don't ask him is because you don't want to see this person as he sees him for obvious reasons, and then again forgive yourself.

Question

Q: I heard you say you forgive yourself. My experience is I can't forgive myself. Would you clarify because I missed it?

K: Strictly speaking we can't forgive ourselves. In the language of the Course, it's the Holy Spirit Who forgives us. What we do is we choose the Holy Spirit, which means we choose against the ego thought system. That's what forgiveness is. It really is a process. As I have been saying all day, a core part of the Course process is asking the Holy Spirit or Jesus for help. The problem is people get that wrong. The asking for help is not for anything external or specific. It is asking for help to look at the ego without judgment. That's forgiveness. That's what it means to forgive one's self. You can't do it by yourself, because what got us into trouble in the first place was doing it by ourselves. It's doing it in the right-minded way, which means that we have joined with the symbol of the right mind, which would be Jesus or the Holy Spirit.

Q: And then the forgiveness is there?

K: Yes, and the act actually of asking for help; that's the forgiveness, because we have already chosen against the ego.

From Darkness to Light **(cont.)**

Let's continue paragraph 5.

(T-11.III.5:1) God hides nothing from His Son, even though His Son would hide himself.

In a sense, this is Jesus' answer to what's expressed in Helen's poems even though Helen's poems were written later. Basically he's saying to Helen, I'm not hiding anything from you. You have hidden yourself from me.

(T-11.III.5:2) Yet the Son of God cannot hide his glory, for God wills him to be glorious, and gave him the light that shines in him.

Once again the problem is we don't believe we are that light. We don't believe we are that glorious Son that God created as Himself. We believe we are creatures of darkness.

(T-11.III.5:3-5) You will never lose your way, for God leads you. When you wander, you but undertake a journey that is not real. [That's the famous Course line: you are on a journey without distance to a goal that has never changed (T-8.VI.9:7).] **The dark companions, the dark way, are all illusions.**

Which is why you don't want to give them power. Not looking at them gives them power, because what's expressed by the not looking is saying these are what I made. These are what are in my mind; they are so awful, so horrific I can't look at them. So I won't look at them. Then I spiritualize it. I'm not going to look at them because they're not real. But you've already made them real. And you know why you have made them real? Because you think you are here. And whenever you say I'm not going to look at them, that's the problem—the "I."

So you are deceiving yourself when you say I'm not going to look at the illusion because it's an illusion. You don't believe it's an illusion because you used the word "I," and you think this course is written for you as a person. It's not written for you as a person. *It's written for you as a decision maker in your mind.* Jesus is not addressing something that doesn't exist.

As I have always said, you can chart your progress in this course to the extent to which you can understand and begin to really experience, so it becomes more than an intellectual idea; that the you that Jesus addresses on every page is not the you that's reading the book or thinks it's reading the book. The you he is addressing is the decision-making part of your mind: the only part that exists in the dream. The part of your mind that chose the ego that must choose again.

But as long as you think you are an "I," then you will think he's talking to you; the person that has a name, that has an identity, a personality. And there's nothing wrong with that. We all begin there. But you want to eventually grow beyond that and make your way up the ladder, so you begin to understand that he's talking to a mind, because that's all there is.

A body doesn't have to change. A body can't change. A puppet doesn't change, and the body is a lifeless piece of wood. There's that line that says who could paint rosy lips upon a skeleton, and then it says pet it and pamper it and make it live (T-23.II.18:8). He's not attacking women for putting on makeup. But he's making the point that just because we dress up our bodies and groom our bodies; we think we are bodies, and we think this is something.

Again, he's not saying not to put on makeup. He's not telling men not to shave. He's not telling us not to take showers or take care of our bodies or see doctors or eat properly, etc. He's simply saying don't have the illusion that this makes you live. He's not talking to us as a body. He's talking to us as a mind.

(T-11.III.5:6-7) Turn toward the light [which means go to your right mind and ask me for help] **for the little spark in you is part of a light so great that it can sweep you out of all darkness forever. For your Father *is* your Creator, and you *are* like Him.**

Meaning the ego is not your creator and you are not like the ego. You are not a separated self. You are not "the home of evil, darkness and sin" (W-pI.93.1:1). You are not a creature of guilt. You remain as God created you.

(T-11.III.6:1-2) The children of light cannot abide in darkness, for darkness is not in them. Do not be deceived by the dark comforters, and never let them enter the mind of God's Son, for they have no place in His temple.

Again, this is the problem. We identify with the body. We identify with what our safety is. "Our safety" is the body that keeps us mindless, which keeps our ego thought system safe and preserves it. Therefore we want to remain in the darkness, and we're afraid of the light. This course, as any other authentic spiritual system, reflects the light. That's why we resist it. That's why a teacher like Jesus is such an ambivalent figure for us. We both love him and hate him. In John's terms, he's both oppressive and he's consummate. And if you don't recognize the negative, you won't be able to enjoy the positive.

(T-11.III.6:3-4) When you are tempted to deny Him [which is anytime we choose separation, anything of the ego] **remember that there *are* no other gods to place before Him, and accept His Will for you in peace. For you cannot accept it otherwise.**

In other words, the ego's thought system, which are our god are the idols of specialness that we worship and bow down to, are not only not there because they are illusory, but they won't work. They will not give us the happiness and peace that we want.

(T-11.III.7:1-2) Only God's Comforter can comfort you. [Not the ego. Not your special love objects.] **In the quiet of His temple, He waits to give you the peace that is yours.**

He's in the temple. He's in our mind. When the Course uses words like temple and altar, Jesus is referring to the mind, specifically the decision-making mind. That's where the altar is. When he talks about altars; that's the altar. And the altar can either be dripping with blood (i.e., the ego's altar), or it can be wreathed with lilies of forgiveness, which is the Holy Spirit's altar. The temple is the mind. We are told, correcting Paul's famous statement, that the temple of the Holy Spirit is *not* a body. It's a relationship, and relationships only exist in the mind.

(T-11.III.7:2-5) ... He waits to give you the peace that is yours. Give His peace, that you may enter the temple and find it waiting for you. [Here is where the tone and the focus shifts to what it means to approach God's temple and to be at His altar.] **But be holy in the Presence of God, or you will**

**not know that you are there. For what is unlike God
cannot enter His Mind, because it was not His Thought
and therefore does not belong to Him.**

What is God's Mind, and what is His Thought? Perfect
Oneness. Which means; if you want to enter God's temple,
and you want to understand and recognize and accept your
own holiness, then you must bring everyone with you. That's
what it means: *But be holy in the Presence of God.* The way
you are holy in the presence of God is not to put yourself in a
state that is antagonistic to His Mind, which is perfect Love
and perfect Oneness. Which means when you come to God's
temple, which is your mind, bring everyone with you, obviously not in form. You bring everyone with you by not
excluding anyone.

The early workbook lessons, which are positively brilliant,
are part of the training to have us understand this statement.
Because the early lessons, if you remember, which seem very
concrete and specific and may even border in your experience
as being trivial, but they are anything but that. They have
you, for example, look around the room; to look at different
objects. And what Jesus says in the instructions, which are
the really important part of the lesson, is *do not exclude
anything.* There's no way you could include everything
because you are only given a couple of minutes to do it.

But he says don't deliberately exclude anything. What
he's beginning for us, is the training to begin to think non-
exclusively. So there's no way, for example, in a group like
this I could talk to everyone for the same amount of time. But
that doesn't mean I exclude certain people and say there are
certain people that I don't want to talk to. You can't have
dinner tonight with everyone. You can't have dinner with
everyone in this room nor with everyone in the world. But in
your mind you don't have to exclude anyone. It's the attitude
of non-exclusivity that the early workbook trains us for, and
that's what he means here.

Be holy in the Presence of God, or you will not know you are there, in the Presence of God is in His temple. And to be holy means to be part of God who is Oneness because that's what holiness is. This doesn't mean you should feel guilty when you find yourself judging and criticizing and excluding people. It simply means don't judge yourself. And be aware, number one, that you are doing it, without either rationalizing it or justifying it. And then understand why you are doing it and the purpose it's serving. Purpose is everything.

You want to exclude certain people because that says the guilt is not in me, it's in them. There's something reprehensible about them. There's something repulsive about them. There is something I don't like about them. There's something bad about them. All that you are saying is there is a spot of darkness in myself I don't want to acknowledge. So I project it out and I see it in these certain people; and then I exclude them. And again, we are not talking about form. We are talking about the content, which is thought. Now this will become clearer as we go along:

(T-11.III.7:7-9) Guard carefully His temple, for He Himself dwells there and abides in peace. You cannot enter God's Presence with the dark companions beside you, but you also cannot enter alone. All your brothers must enter with you, for until you have accepted them *you* cannot enter.

That is a very, very clear statement. When Jesus says *guard carefully His temple,* he's really elaborating on the third lesson of the Holy Spirit in Chapter 6 to be vigilant only for God and His Kingdom (T-6.V-C). He's not saying that God needs a defense. He's saying in your mind you should be vigilant for your attraction to the ego and its thought system and the dark companions. *You cannot enter God's Presence with the dark companions*: the ego thought system of specialness. You cannot enter alone; you must bring everyone with you.

Skip quickly to the next page, 201, paragraph 5, sentence 6 in italics.

(T-11.IV.5:6) *You cannot enter God's Presence if you attack His Son.*

Skip now to paragraph 6:

(T-11.IV.6:1-2) Christ is at God's altar, waiting to welcome His Son. But come wholly without condemnation, for otherwise you will believe that the door is barred and you cannot enter.

Which means if you attack any aspect of the Sonship, it's because you do not want to enter God's temple. And then you will project the blame out and say God is not there. Jesus is not there. Everything is purposive. If you criticize someone, mildly criticize someone or say something very mildly, tangentially, indirectly, subtly attacking, it is deliberate. Because your ego knows, the part of you that likes being yourself knows that if you exclude this person, you are safe, because you can't enter God's light unless you bring everyone with you.

Your dishonesty then starts when you say the reason I don't feel God's peace is either because God is not there, this course doesn't work, Jesus lied to me, or this S.O.B. did it to me again. It's all a lie. Helen's poems, as wonderfully evocative as they are to describe the dark night, are lies. Jesus did not betray her. He did not break his promise. She broke hers, and then the guilt gets projected out.

Again what's instructive about those poems is not only how it unveils this darkness that's in all of us, but it also unveils the ego's secret trick. I exist, I'm miserable, and I'm unhappy. But it's not my fault. Someone else did it to me. So again going back now to page 200, paragraph 7, I will read sentence 9 again.

(T-11.III.7:9-10) All your brothers must enter with you, for until you have accepted them *you* cannot enter. For you cannot understand wholeness unless you are whole, and no part of the Son can be excluded if he would know the Wholeness of his Father.

Christ passes no one by and thus you know He is God's Son. This basically is the bottom line of every talk anyone ever should give on this course, because this is what it comes down to. Beware of the temptation to perceive yourself unfairly treated (T-26.X.4:1); to blame someone else.

You cannot understand wholeness unless you are whole, and no part of the Son can be excluded if he would know the Wholeness of his Father. Which means, once again, if you exclude anyone, it's because you don't want to know the wholeness of your Father. Because in the wholeness of your Father, you as an individual, differentiated, separated consciousness do not exist. So to preserve that self, you choose to protect yourself by separating from love and wholeness and then blaming someone else for it. See that each and every time you harbor an unloving thought, and then stop. Forgiveness is still. It quietly does nothing, and merely looks, and waits, and judges not (W-pII.I.4.1,3).

But call a spade a spade. This is what I'm doing. This is why I'm doing it, and at least now I can accept responsibility for why I feel the absence of God's Love. Now I can understand why I don't understand this course. These lines are very clear. No one could not understand them, unless they did not want to understand them. This helps you understand why you don't want to understand. Because they are so clear and they are so simple. It's the simplicity and the clarity and the directness that is so frightening.

Our egos give a message to our eyes and to our brains, *"Don't see this."* Or we go into brain fog or become brain dead and don't understand it, because it is very, very clear. All you need to do is just be aware of it and not judge yourself for it, and say I'm simply afraid of the wholeness. I'm afraid of love, and that's okay.

But I'm told not to be afraid that I will be abruptly lifted up and hurled into reality (T-16.VI.8:1). I will not forgive one day and the next day disappear into the Heart of God. I will forgive one day and the next day and the day after that. And in time, I will be less lonely, less angry, less anxious, less guilty, less depressed, more loving, kinder, more peaceful, more concerned with other people, and more caring. What's wrong with that?

There's nothing wrong with that except part of you knows, if I take those steps, and then a few steps after that will follow and will follow and will follow; and before you know it, I'm living totally in the present without a past. And that's frightening, because that means I don't have a future that I have to be afraid of. And I gradually find myself going higher and higher on the ladder, and before I know it, I'm home. And that's the fear.

"Arise with Me"

I want to read three poems that are exactly the opposite of what I've read to you. The first is called "Arise With Me." This was written a month or two before those dark night poems. Actually it was written on New Year's Day. It's page 46. As with most of the poems and certainly all of the poems that I've read to you and will read to you today, Jesus is the one who is being addressed. This now is more reflective of the state of what John was writing about after the night. In other words, what the night led to. These poems reflect Helen's right mind and, therefore, reflect everyone's right mind.

> O You who came in winter and who left
> Among the lilies, stay with me and fill

> My eyes with glory, and my heart with love
> That smiles forever on the world You saw,
> And that You loved as You would have me love.
> For with this vision I will look on You,
> And recognize my Savior in all things
> I did not understand. Now is the world
> Reborn in me because I share Your Love.
> Now in my healed and holy mind there dawns
> The memory of God. And now I rise
> To Him in all the loveliness I knew
> When I was first created one with You.
> *(The Gifts of God,* p. 46)

What you find in this poem is a number of very, very important themes in the Course. And actually it touches upon another important theme in John of the Cross. You don't find that in the poems I read to you, but he was very big on the idea that once you have that experience of Jesus' love, then everything you look on in the world will be filled with God's Love. Now he certainly did not believe the world was an illusion. So for him, God created the world, but that you then saw everything in the world as reflecting God's Love. So when Helen says here:

For with this vision I will look on You, [meaning Jesus]
And recognize my Savior in all things
I did not understand.

She will look on everything in the world that beforehand she had misunderstood. Seeing it as something separate from her, she would now realize that everything now was seen through the eyes of Jesus' love, which meant everything was the same.

What amounts to a formula in this course is that you see the face of Christ in your brother and remember God. In other words, once you forgive and forgive totally, which is what seeing the face of Christ in your brother means, then all that's left is a split second when the memory of God dawns in your mind. In other words the ego's out of the way, and all that's left is this thought, which is the Holy Spirit that reminds us of who we are. You see the face of Christ in your brother, which means you see that face of innocence in everyone.

You recognize your Savior in all things you did not understand. And with the ego out of the way, then the memory of God dawns in your mind and everything is finished. And so that's what she is saying here. And then:

> [In her] **healed and holy mind there dawns**
> **The memory of God. And now I rise**
> **To Him** [meaning God] **in all the loveliness I knew**
> **When I was first created one with You** [meaning Jesus].

There's no difference now between her and Jesus. We're all One. We're all part of God's One Son. In the imagery of John's poems, the lover and the Beloved become One. And in that love and in that Oneness, all of creation shines with that love.

In the Course's specific theory, in that love, which is only in the mind; that love flows throughout the whole Sonship, which is one mind. And then when your eyes look out, they look out only from the perspective of that love within your mind, and everything and everyone is bathed in that love. No matter what their bodies are doing, everything is bathed in that love.

"Love Song"

The last two poems I want to read are two of the Valentine's Day poems, "Love Song," and "The Resting Place." They're pages 53 and 54. As I have mentioned other times, this was a time when I started nudging Helen that I thought it might be nice if she wrote love poems to Jesus as a way of counteracting a lot of those other poems. I started in January and said Valentine's Day is coming. I think it would be really nice if you wrote him a Valentine's poem. She ended up writing three poems. I'll read you the first two of those three poems.

Basically again, just as John's poems are really love poems to Jesus, these two poems are quite clearly love poems to Jesus as well, without the kind of imagery you find in John. This first is called "Love Song."

> My Lord, my Love, my Life, I live in you.
> There is no life apart from what you are.
> I breathe your words, I rest upon your arms.
> My sight is hallowed by your single star.
>
> I do not always recognize your face,
> Or hear your Voice. I do not always see
> The strangers whom you send are messengers
> You choose to bring your holy Word to me.
>
> You are the stranger then. And I am dead
> To holy things that Heaven's light shines through.
> The world I see is enemy to me
> When I forget my lovely Love is you.
>
> Forgetting you is to forget myself,
> Why I have come and where it is I go.
> My Lord, my Love, my Life, let me forget
> All things except the loveliness you know.
> (*The Gifts of God*, p. 53)

John would have loved this poem, especially that last line:

My Lord, my Love, my Life, let me forget
All things except the loveliness you know.

Let me forget everything, which is nothing. Once I realize everything is nothing, what remains is the everything of my love for you. And in this poem, you do find the identification of Helen with Jesus, just as you find that in John's poetry. "Forgetting you is to forget myself," because your love is who I am.

There is a lovely medieval German anonymous statement that says, "I have nothing, I want nothing, I am nothing but the love of Jesus." *I have nothing, I want nothing, I am nothing but the love of Jesus.* And we're not talking about Jesus the man. We're not talking about Jesus as a theological figure. We are talking about a Jesus who represents the Love of God in everyone's right mind.

Once again, to be sure, there are many, many other symbols of God's Love, but certainly in the Western world, he is *the* predominant symbol. To profess love for him is not to profess love to an historical person, which makes no sense. We profess love to a part of us that we have excluded that his love represents for us. And that's what this love poem is really about.

Another very, very important aspect of it is in the second stanza. "I do not always see the strangers whom you send are messengers you choose to bring your holy Word to me." Those of you who know the *Psychotherapy* pamphlet that Helen had taken down, it closes with how very simple are the ways of salvation. *"You were lost in the darkness of the world until you asked for light. And then God sent His Son to give it to you"* (P-3.III.8:12-13). And God's Son is not Jesus. You were lost in the darkness of your own guilt, and the way to undo your guilt is to see someone that you have excluded, that you projected your guilt onto, and to realize that the Light of Christ shines in that person just as it shines in you.

That's the Course's way of salvation and that's what Helen is expressing here; that I did not realize that the people in my life are messengers. Not that Jesus sent them to us. He's not a chess player that moves pieces around the board. But everyone in our lives is a potential messenger. Obviously everyone in our life *is* a messenger. Our choice is whether they will be messengers of guilt and darkness, or messengers of love and light. Because everyone who comes into our life, we project onto. That is inevitable. That is what minds do. Minds project. By watching how I react to you, I can tell the difference whether I'm seeing you through the eyes of my ego or through the loving eyes of Jesus. If I'm angry with you or critical of you, if I see you as special, if I make you different from me, then obviously it's my ego doing that. And this is my opportunity now to accept God's Word; and in the Course, God's Word is Atonement or forgiveness.

When I don't do that and I exclude someone, then you are the stranger then. *And I am dead to holy things that Heaven's light shines through. The world I see is enemy to me when I forget my lovely Love is you.* When you realize that the one we love is him and that love is us, there's no way we could exclude anyone. But when we exclude someone, once again, it's because we want to exclude that love, because we want to see ourselves as creations of hate and guilt and darkness rather than of love and light.

"The Resting Place"

The final poem, which I will just read, and then we will stop is called "The Resting Place." Actually there was an alternate title. Helen originally called it "In Joyous Welcome," which is a phrase which is in the poem. But "The Resting Place" actually I think is nicer. I'll comment on the poem first this time, and then I will read it straight through.

This poem expresses again how lost we are without him. *Without you I'm lost in senseless wanderings that have no end.* And that's the darkness. That's the dark night, when we leave without him. When we join with him, then the darkness turns into light because we look at everything and everyone through his eyes. And when we join with him again, as this poem ends: *the journey is forgotten in the joy of endless quiet and your kiss of peace.*

Everything ends. All the pain, all the suffering, all the angst, all the despair, all the anger, all of it disappears. And all that is required is that we walk the path with him, which means we walk the path with our right-minded self. But since we are a symbol of the wrong-minded self, then we need a figure like a Jesus to represent that right-minded self. And when we take his hand and he leads us through the labyrinth of hate and guilt and fear; his love, while it accompanies us, is also on the other side. When we reach that other side, everything ends. And that's what this poem means, and we rest in him just as John rested in the arms of his Beloved.

> My arms are open. Come, my Lord, to me
> And rest upon my heart. It beats for you
> And sings in joyous welcome. What am I
> Except your resting place and your repose?
>
> Your rest is mine. Without you I am lost
> In senseless wanderings that have no end,
> No goal, no meaning, on a road that goes
> In twisted byways down to nothingness.
>
> Come now, my Love, and save me from despair.
> The Way, the Truth, the Life are with me then.
> The journey is forgotten in the joy
> Of endless quiet and your kiss of peace.
> (*The Gifts of God*, p. 54)

ST. JOHN OF THE CROSS
(available as a pdf download at
https://facim.org/online-learning-aids/st-john-of-the-cross)

The Dark Night

One dark night,
fired with love's urgent longings
- ah, the sheer grace! -
I went out unseen,
my house being now all stilled.

In darkness, and secure,
by the secret ladder, disguised,
- ah, the sheer grace! -
in darkness and concealment,
my house being now all stilled.

On that glad night,
in secret, for no one saw me,
nor did I look at anything,
with no other light or guide
than the one that burned in my heart.

This guided me
more surely than the light of noon
to where he was awaiting me
- him I knew so well -
there in a place where no one appeared.

O guiding night!
O night more lovely than the dawn!
O night that has united
the Lover with his beloved,
transforming the beloved in her Lover.

Upon my flowering breast
which I kept wholly for him alone,
there he lay sleeping,
and I caressing him
there in a breeze from the fanning cedars.

When the breeze blew from the turret,
as I parted his hair,
it wounded my neck
with its gentle hand,
suspending all my senses.

I abandoned and forgot myself,
laying my face on my Beloved;
all things ceased; I went out from myself,
leaving my cares
forgotten among the lilies.

The Living Flame of Love

O living flame of love
that tenderly wounds my soul
in its deepest center! Since
now you are not oppressive,
now consummate! if it be your will:
tear through the veil of this sweet encounter!

O sweet cautery,
O delightful wound!
O gentle hand! O delicate touch
that tastes of eternal life
and pays every debt!
In killing you changed death to life.

O lamps of fire!
in whose splendors
the deep caverns of feeling,
once obscure and blind,
now give forth, so rarely, so exquisitely,
both warmth and light to their Beloved.

How gently and lovingly
you wake in my heart,
where in secret you dwell alone;
and in your sweet breathing,
filled with good and glory,
how tenderly you swell my heart with love.

"The Glory of the Infinite"

Introduction

The title for today is "The Glory of the Infinite." That's a phrase that comes right near the end of "The Gifts of God" prose poem. It's a very moving ending. I'll describe that and discuss that later in the workshop. We'll actually read that as a closing. It's used there basically as a way of describing Heaven. I'll read you just a little bit of it. It's used synonymously with the joy of Heaven and the holy peace of earth, and then all this is returned to us.

There's not very much in the Course that describes what Heaven is like or the state of infinity is like because, as Jesus says at one point, it's merely "senseless musings" to try to understand something that there's no way we could understand (W-pI.139.8:5). But there are several passages throughout that point to what Heaven is like or the infinite is like. I thought I'd start by reading one of them. It's in the text, page 194 and we'll start with paragraph 2.

(T-11.I.2:1) To be alone is to be separated from infinity, but how can this be if infinity has no end? No one can be beyond the limitless, because what has no limits must be everywhere. There are no beginnings and no endings in God, Whose universe is Himself. Can you exclude yourself from the universe, or from God Who *is* the universe? I [that, of course, is Jesus. I] and my Father are one with you, for you are part of Us. Do you really believe that part of God can be missing or lost to Him?

(T-11.I.3) If you were not part of God, His Will would not be unified. Is this conceivable? Can part of His Mind contain nothing? If your place in His Mind cannot be filled by anyone except you, and your filling it was your creation, without you there would be an empty place in

God's Mind. Extension cannot be blocked, and it has no voids. It continues forever, however much it is denied. Your denial of its reality may arrest it in time, but not in eternity. That is why your creations have not ceased to be extended, and why so much is waiting for your return.

(T-11.I.4) Waiting is possible only in time, but time has no meaning. You who made delay can leave time behind simply by recognizing that neither beginnings nor endings were created by the Eternal, Who placed no limits on His creation or upon those who create like Him. You do not know this simply because you have tried to limit what He created, and so you believe that all creation is limited. How, then, could you know your creations, having denied infinity?

There's no way, as we're told in many other places in the Course, we could really understand an experience, a realm of being that has no beginning and no ending, that is timeless, that is infinite. The reason we can't is because we have made ourselves to be creatures of the finite. To be creatures who are limited, creatures who are separated, who are differentiated one from the other; the exact opposite of the glory of the infinite or the state of Heaven. And so the problem is that we find ourselves as creatures of the finite. How could we possibly understand what infinity is?

What I want to do with you today is actually divide this talk into three parts. What I've just been talking about is the introduction. What I will actually begin the workshop with is really talking about what the finite is. And to use a horrible play on words, we'll talk about *the gory of the finite* rather than *the glory of the infinite*, because that's where we begin. There's no way that we can get from the finite to the infinite without some intermediate steps. And the figure that best represents that intermediate step would be Jesus.

The second part of what I'll be talking about this afternoon will be Jesus and his role of being the bridge, as he himself says at the beginning of the text (T-1.II.4). He is the bridge between the finite and the infinite, between the illusion and the truth. And then finally we will talk about the glory of the infinite and what it really means to return home, from which we never left.

The Infinite

Let me speak a little bit more about what the infinite is. Let me read you a couple other passages to get us started. The next one is in the text page 246, the bottom of the page, paragraph 7. It's the section called "The Function of Time."

(T-13.IV.7:1-5) It is evident that the Holy Spirit's perception of time is the exact opposite of the ego's. The reason is equally clear, for they perceive the goal of time as diametrically opposed. The Holy Spirit interprets time's purpose as rendering the need for time unnecessary. He regards the function of time as temporary, serving only His teaching function, which is temporary by definition. His emphasis is therefore on the only aspect of time that can extend to the infinite, for *now* is the closest approximation of eternity that this world offers.

Now, of course, would be synonymous with the holy instant. That's the instant outside of time and space when our mind shifts from the ego as its teacher to the Holy Spirit or Jesus as its Teacher. That's the instant when we choose to forgive rather than condemn; to be healed rather than to be sickened by guilt; and to embrace love instead of to have embraced fear.

(T-13.IV.7:6-7) It is in the reality of "now," without past or future, that the beginning of the appreciation of eternity lies. For only "now" is here, and only "now" presents the opportunities for the holy encounters in which salvation can be found.

This really is the bridge between the illusion and the truth. It's practicing the holy instant. It's learning forgiveness from Jesus, who is its teacher. It's taking the little steps, as the end of Lesson 193 says. It's taking the little steps that God asks us to take to him (W-pI.193.13:7).

Once again, and I'll come back to this over and over again today, one does not go from the finite to the infinite. One does not go from the gore of the ego's thought system, and all the cruelty and the misery and the suffering and the pain of being in the ego's thought system, first in the mind and then in the world, without an intermediate step that gently leads us from that gore to the glory. And, one more time, Jesus represents for us that great symbol of that bridge.

The Changeless Dwelling Place

The final passage that I want to read is relatively near the end of the text. It's page 614 in the text. It's the section called "The Changeless Dwelling Place." This is a beautiful section. We'll just read the opening two paragraphs. This is really reflecting this glorious state of being in the infinite, which is where God created us, our true Self.

(T-29.V.1) **There is a place in you where this whole world has been forgotten; where no memory of sin and of illusion lingers still. There is a place in you which time has left, and echoes of eternity are heard. There is a resting place so still no sound except a hymn to Heaven rises up to gladden God the Father and the Son. Where Both abide are They remembered, Both. And where They are is Heaven and is peace.**

(T-29.V.2) **Think not that you can change Their dwelling place. For your Identity abides in Them, and**

where They are, forever must you be. The changelessness of Heaven is in you, so deep within that nothing in this world but passes by, unnoticed and unseen. The still infinity of endless peace surrounds you gently in its soft embrace, so strong and quiet, tranquil in the might of its Creator, nothing can intrude upon the sacred Son of God within.

Well, the problem, of course, is that we did believe we could change Their dwelling place, the "Their" being God and Christ. And that's when the infinite suddenly became the finite.

The Finite

Let me read you another passage from the same chapter, which will usher in our discussion of the finite. It's page 620 also in the text, the bottom of the page, paragraph 6. This is the section called "The Anti-Christ," which of course has nothing to do with the devil as is taught in Christian tradition. The anti-Christ is the ego, which is literally "anti," against Christ; the ego being the total opposite of Heaven; its thought system of separation, differentiation, judgment and attack being the exact opposite of Heaven's state of perfect Oneness and perfect love. The ego now becomes the self which stands in opposition to this glorious Self of Christ that God created. That's the anti-Christ.

A major symbol that the Course uses near the end of the text, and we see it certainly here is "idol." Actually, it occurs earlier too in the text, but it becomes even more strongly used here. Idol would be a synonym for our special relationships. These are the idols that we establish that substitute for God.

Basically when we engage on our endless pursuit of love in this world, which of course is special love, we're saying

God's Love is not enough for me. The love that Jesus holds out to me is not enough. Instead, I want this special love that this special person with these special attributes can give me. It doesn't even have to be a person. It can be a pet, it can be a plant, it can be a substance like alcohol or drugs, food. It can be a cause; it can be anything and everything in the world that we believe will complete us and make us whole. That's the idol.

So paragraph 6 begins actually with that:

(T-29.VIII.6:1) An idol is established by belief [meaning that it's our decision-making mind's belief in the ego that establishes the seeming reality of the ego, and then of the idols that the ego has made]**, and when it is withdrawn the idol "dies."**

When our decision-making mind realizes that it chose the wrong teacher and identified with the wrong thought system; that thought system disappears. The word "dies" is put in quotes because it doesn't die. To have something die means that it lived and means that it existed. Well, the ego never existed. It only existed in our deluded minds that believed that the thought system of separation was real.

(T-29.VIII.6:1-3) An idol is established by belief, and when it is withdrawn the idol "dies." This is the anti-Christ; the strange idea [now this is what happened in that insane moment; that tiny, mad idea when we believed as one Son that we could separate from our Creator and Source. This is what happened; the strange idea] **there is a power past omnipotence, a place beyond the infinite, a time transcending the eternal. Here the world of idols has been set by the idea this power and place and time are given form, and shape the world where the impossible has happened.**

Now what is described here in poetic terms is really the entirety of what happened in that original moment. In that original moment when we believed there could be *a power past omnipotence, and a place beyond the infinite, and time came to take the place of the eternal,* the ego's thought system was born and our individual identity was born. We identified with that self and embraced it. And it became real because of our embrace of it, not because there was anything that we were embracing. How could you embrace nothing? Then in order to protect that newborn self which could easily be extinguished by the same power of mind that gave it reality—namely, our belief in it; in order to ensure that we could never change our belief in it, this whole thought system was projected out and made up a world, literally. Both on the macrocosmic level that there was a physical universe or cosmos; and then the microcosmic level because that original thought system fragmented and scattered itself into billions and billions and billions and billions of pieces. Microcosmically, that thought system projected out, gave rise to our individual existence as bodies; and macrocosmically, it gave birth to the entire cosmos.

So that's what this means.

(T-29.VIII.6:3-4) Here the world of idols has been set by the idea this power and place and time are given form, and shape the world where the impossible has happened. Here the deathless come to die...

This is now talking about the world of bodies. And since we have forgotten where the world came from, we actually believe there's a world here; a world of bodies in which the inherently deathless, because we are eternal as spirit, come to die. I usually quote the line from Part II of the workbook that the world is a dry and dusty place in which starved and thirsty creatures come to die (W-pII.13.5:1). And of course, once you understand this, then it becomes absurd that we let the world affect us; that we let the world take our peace away from us, let the world upset us; that we let other people's insane egos (that mirror our insane ego's) affect us.

105

What we relive every single moment when we allow anything and everything in the world to affect us is we relive that original moment when we believed there was a power past omnipotence; that there is a place beyond the infinite. And there's now a world of time instead of the world of eternity. Even though it's not talked about here, it's when hate takes the place of love, when fear takes the place of love, when specialness takes the place of perfect Oneness.

Perfect love and perfect peace are within us. That memory of that love and oneness is at the core of our right minds. That's what the Holy Spirit is. Every time we allow ourselves to be upset, we are denying that love and Oneness and saying there is a power past omnipotence. The omnipotence of Heaven has nothing to do with power in the world's sense. It's not a question of domination or oppressing people or subjugating people to your will. It's the power of perfect love, which is totally unified and embraces all seemingly separated fragments and aspects of that love as One; what the Course refers to as a "Oneness joined as One" (T-25.I.7:1).

Each and every time we become upset, we let the finite determine us, we let the finite affect us, we let the finite change us from created beings of love to guilt-ridden creatures of the ego. So again:

(T-29.VIII.6:4) Here the deathless come to die, the all-encompassing to suffer loss, the timeless to be made the slaves of time.

One of the grand illusions of this world, grand from the ego's point of view is that we age and we die because these are the laws of the body. These are the laws of nature. These are the laws of time. But that's not why we age. We age because we believe there's *a power past omnipotence, a place beyond the infinite,* a world of time instead of a world of eternity. That's why we age. How could what God created as perfect as Himself age? How could it change?

The title of the section I just read from before was called "The Changeless Dwelling Place." Well, you know this world is not your home because everything here changes. One of the great lies of the 2+2=4 world is that people change because of the laws of nature, because of the laws of time. That could only be, just to say it again, because you believe there's *a power past omnipotence, a place beyond the infinite*, and a world of time instead of the world of eternity: a place of hate and fear and pain instead of a place of love and peace.

(T-29.VIII.6:5-6) Here does the changeless change; the peace of God, forever given to all living things, give way to chaos. And the Son of God, as perfect, sinless and as loving as his Father, come to hate a little while; to suffer pain and finally to die.

That's our great and wonderful world. That's the world of bodies that people seek to preserve and fight to preserve and try to cheat the laws of death, and live longer and longer and longer. *And the Son of God, as perfect, sinless and as loving as his Father, come to hate a little while; to suffer pain and finally to die.*

Each and every time you have any thought that is not of perfect love and perfect peace, this is what you're subscribing to; everything I just read to you in paragraph 6. In other words, we all end up worshipping idols instead of accepting the Christ in us. We all become disciples of the anti-Christ. And once again, we're not talking about the devil. We become disciples of the anti-Christ.

All this is highlighted even more in the next paragraph.

(T-29.VIII.7) Where is an idol? Nowhere! Can there be a gap in what is infinite, a place where time can interrupt eternity? A place of darkness set where all is light, a dismal alcove separated off from what is endless, *has* no place to be. An idol is beyond where God has set all things forever,

and has left no room for anything to be except His Will. Nothing and nowhere must an idol be, while God is everything and everywhere.

The problem, of course, is that we have identified with the "nothing" and with the "nowhere." What is very, very helpful as you practice this course is to realize without guilt and without judgment and without any self-condemnation; but recognize that each and every time you experience anything other than perfect love and perfect peace for all people and all things, you are identifying with paragraphs 6 and 7, as well as a lot of other places in the Course. You are saying I believe in the nothingness of nowhere. I believe I live in the nowhere of nothingness.

I sometimes kid about the section in the clarification of terms on the ego which purports to clarify the terms the Course uses. And of course, it doesn't do that really. It just describes them beautifully. In the one on the ego, it says, what is the ego? Nothing. Where is the ego? Nowhere (C-2.6). That's not very helpful. And that's juxtaposed with the miracle. And then it says, what is the miracle? The exact opposite of the ego (C-2.5,7). Well, that's taken from what I just read to you.

(T-29.VIII.7:5-6) ... God has set all things forever, and has left no room for anything to be except His Will. Nothing and nowhere must an idol be, while God is everything and everywhere.

As we all know, the problem in all this is that we are creatures of the finite. We are creatures of the nothing and the nowhere. Somewhere deep within us is that awareness, even if it's not conscious that if we choose the road that takes us back to the Everything and the Everywhere, we will cease to exist as finite entities. That's the problem. That's why, as we're told many different places, we don't go from nightmares to reality. We're not abruptly lifted up and hurled into reality (T-16.VI.8:1). We go slowly, step by step.

As horrendous as it sounds and as it seems, we are all attracted to the gore of the finite. To the ego, the infinite is gory. We are all attracted to it because it's that thought system that gave rise to us. That's why an understanding of the Course's metaphysics is so important and passages like this are so important, especially when you juxtapose them with the passages I read at the beginning that describe what Heaven is like and what the infinite is like.

If the infinite alone is what is true, then anything that is finite only exists for the purpose of hiding the memory of the infinite. If only the infinite is true and only the infinite is our Identity, and if the glory of the infinite, which is God's Son, is who we are, then anything that is not of that glory, which must be shared with everyone; that must be reflective of the perfect Oneness of Heaven—everything that is not that glorious infinite, cannot be real.

What happens over years of study of the Course is that as you go through your day you become increasingly aware of your cherishing of specialness and not wanting to let it go. And you become aware of all the petty hates and the silly grievances that you hold onto and you won't let go; that you catch yourself fantasizing about special love objects or special hate objects, dreaming of vengeance or plotting the next person you're going to cannibalize. These thoughts go on all the time in our wrong minds. As you catch yourself doing that, realize that these are purposive.

Look at the next line, paragraph 8.

(T-29.VIII.8:1-4) What purpose has an idol, then? What is it for? This is the only question that has many answers, each depending on the one of whom the question has been asked. The world believes in idols.

What's now going on is that we all have different purposes here. But what is really important is to ask: why do I do this? What is the purpose that worshipping idols serves for me? Why can't I let go of this anger? Why can't I let go of continually bringing the past in to inform my present experience? Why do I keep dreaming all my special love fantasies? This time it'll be different. This time God will be there. This relationship will really last and be meaningful. Why do you still cherish all these illusions? *Because it preserves our finite identity.*

If this identity is real, and the world in which this identity finds its home is real, then the underlying thought system must be real as well. The thought system of separation, of sin, of guilt and fear must be real, and all the gore of the ego's finite thought system. If all of that is real, then it means God is not, which means my identity is preserved seemingly forever, even beyond the grave. That's why people have an idea of an afterlife and then of a hell, of course. This preserves the individual self.

We can't move beyond the finite to the infinite until we recognize, number one, what the finite is, what the world of the finite is, what the world of specialness is. Only then can we meaningfully ask for help.

This course is a totally self-contained curriculum. You don't need anything else but the three books. And it comes fully equipped with a teacher. The batteries may not be included but the teacher is included. [Laughter] A teacher is no good if you don't welcome the teacher into your classroom. What good is a teacher if the teacher teaches in a classroom down the hall when you're in this classroom? You have to welcome the teacher into your classroom and that classroom is your life and all the relationships in your life. And you have to know what it is you want to study. Because if you want to study A and your teacher is teaching B, no learning will occur.

What our teacher is presenting us with is a curriculum of forgiveness based on our curriculum of unforgiveness. But if we're not interested in learning forgiveness, we're not going to learn anything. There's that section early on in the text, "The Direction of the Curriculum" (T-8.I), which focuses on the frustration and inability to learn when you're pursuing two different curriculums with two different teachers, each going in the opposite direction. The ego's notion of forgiveness is totally opposite from the Holy Spirit's notion of forgiveness. The ego's notion of joining is always of the body. Jesus' notion of joining is always of the mind.

There's no way we can learn when we're always being pulled in opposite directions. But before we can avail ourselves of the wisdom of our teacher, we first have to recognize what it is we want to learn. In other words, we have to realize and experience being fed up with the ego thought system, becoming fully aware that it just doesn't work. It doesn't make us happy. It does not give us the peace of God. It does not bring us closer to home. If anything, it drives us still further away from home, even more deeply into the arms of the finite, which the ego tells us is glorious.

Special love feels so wonderful. We all live for that special love high, whether it's with a person, whether it's with food, whether it's with a substance, whether it's victory on a sports field or in the political arena, it doesn't matter. There's a high. That's what we live for. And the ego tells us, that's glorious.

That's why it's really helpful to continue to juxtapose what the Course tells us is the reality and then describes over and over again what the illusion is. Reality is changeless. It is eternal. It doesn't deteriorate. It doesn't age. It doesn't live. It doesn't die. It doesn't judge. It doesn't attack. It doesn't hold onto the past. It doesn't live as if the past were real.

There's that workbook lesson, "The past is over. It can touch me not" (W-pII.289). But we still cling to memories of the past and use it to justify our present decisions to separate from another person. We're all masters of that because we're creatures of linear time. And we actually think that the past has an effect on us. Once again, we think that the world's laws have an effect on us; that we age because of certain laws of nature, without realizing that the so-called laws of nature

111

are most unnatural. The only natural law is the changelessness of Heaven, the changelessness of Christ. The only reality is the glory of the infinite.

We have to realize that this world is a crucifixion; that this world really is *a dry and dusty place where starved and thirsty creatures come to die.* If we don't realize that, we will never be motivated to choose against it and say there must be another way. There must be another teacher. There must be another world. As the workbook says, beyond this world there's another world, another world I want to see (W-pI. 129.7:3); a world of forgiveness, a world of true learning, which the Course tells us is unlearning. But we have to be motivated to learn. We have to recognize what the finite world really is like.

"Holy Saturday"

Since we're going to be talking about Jesus in a moment, I want to read one of Helen's poems. This is a gory poem. This is not a very nice poem, but it describes what this world is like. If we don't recognize what the world is like, we'll never be able to hear the lovely poems that Helen took down and really identify with them. This poem is called "Holy Saturday" (*The Gifts of God*, p.108).

For those of you who do not know much about Christianity, Holy Saturday is the day between Good Friday and Easter Sunday. Holy Saturday is when it seems absolutely nothing is meaningful anymore. All of the hopes that the world had or that the disciples had in terms of Jesus—we're going by the gospel stories only now—were crushed on the day of crucifixion. Holy Saturday is that interim day between the seeming death of Jesus on the cross and then his resurrection on Sunday. It's a day of utter hopelessness and despair. It's the traditional Christian expression of the dark night of the soul, when all of the hopes that something would work, that specialness would finally come through, that there could be a special body that would come to help us and save us—all of these were dashed.

Basically what this poem expresses in much larger terms is what everyone's individual experience is when, once again, the special relationship fails us, and we're left with the despair of realizing nothing works. What's implied in this very evocative poem is obviously a real condemnation of Jesus and basically blaming Jesus that he didn't keep his word. This seems to be the glorification of the ego thought system. The ego finally has emerged triumphant. It defeated God. It defeated love. It defeated salvation and smashed it into smithereens.

This is what this world is like. We all come into this world with the hope, this time it'll be different. When people laughingly talk about the innocence of children, and I say laughingly because children are far from innocent; but when people talk about the innocence of children, what they're really talking about is the innocence that believes this time it will work. This time the body will work. This time I'll get what I want. This time my needs will be satisfied. I'll find the perfect relationship, the perfect Mommy and Daddy, the perfect friend, the perfect lover, the perfect spouse. I'll have the perfect children. I'll have the perfect job. I'll have the perfect body. I'll finally find God.

Then as we grow older, if we're really honest, we would realize, I'll never find God here. I'll never find true love here. I'll never find genuine peace here. We go through life having one despairing experience after another. But we don't quit, and we just keep trying to make it different. "This time it'll happen. I know how to play the game now." We don't want to realize that this is *a dry and dusty world where starved and thirsty creatures come to die.* So this is what this poem expresses.

> The door is solid. Ancient keys are gone.
> The rusted hinge stands firm. The bolt is shut,
> And spiders' castles shimmer in the gleam
> Of tired moonlight.

This is the ego's world. This is the underside of when it appears to be that special love is working.

> Everything seems put
> In place forever, and decay has come
> To wage a ceaseless war against the hope
> Of sunlight. What was once a window stands
> Like blackness in the dark. My fingers grope
> Along the walls and bleed on granite thorns.
> I would not hear You knock.

The "You" would be Jesus. We are so enveloped in the darkness of despair that even if he were to knock on this door that is solid and all the keys are gone, we would not hear him. "I would not hear You knock." "Would" also has the meaning that I don't want to hear You knock.

Other times I've mentioned Helen's, also very evocative poem, "Stranger on the Road" (*The Gifts of God*, p. 103), which is based on the resurrection story from the gospel where Jesus appears to his disciples on the road to Emmaus after his crucifixion, and they don't recognize him at first. In the poem Helen knows who he is in the poem and says, "I don't want to see you. Don't disturb me. I don't want to see that you're here, because if you're here then it means everything that my life rests on is a lie." Everything my life rests on is the ego thought system that culminates in death. And if death is not real and if you, Jesus, are really here, then everything I believed in is not true. That's what this means.

> I would not hear you knock. The air is thin,
> And whistles through the small remaining gap
> Upon the dark that lets the moon's edge in.

**I fell so long ago I could not come
To let You enter, even if I heard
You knock against the door.** [In other words that
death is coming. I don't even have the energy
now to choose life.] **I could not reach
The crumbling handle, nor could speak the word
Of welcome that would ask You enter and
Abide with me.**

In other words, all hope is gone; all faith is gone. People
are very much tempted to do the same thing with *A Course in
Miracles.* You get the Course and there's a honeymoon
period where you think, "Oh, this is the answer to everything.
This will save me, it'll save the world." And then you begin
to realize that what this course really does is shine a light on
your ego, on your "hidden hates" and "secret sins" (T-31.
VIII.9:2). *And that's unbearable.* That's when the special
love for the Course turns into special hate.

And then we accuse the Course of failing us, of being
written in such a way we couldn't possibly understand it. Or
that it's in a language that we find unacceptable. It's too
Christian, it's too male sexist, it's too this, it's too that. But
we become too, too weak, which means we believe the ego
has won. And the weakness that we feel is really the triumphant strength of the ego. It has defeated God again. It has
defeated eternal life. As the text says near the end, it has
chosen our weakness instead of the strength of Christ (T-31.
VIII.2:3).

When we play weak and we play inadequate and vulnerable and deficient in certain ways, that's the ego's strength. It
seems to be weakness. It's really strength. It's standing up
before God and saying, "You see? I exist outside of your
perfect strength and your perfect Love and your perfect
Oneness." That takes real strength. It's not weakness. It's the
strength of defiance. It's the strength of proving that you're
right and God is wrong. Even here in this poem, in the

weakness of despair, really underlying that is this great strength.

> **Your light** [again, the "you" that's addressed is Jesus]
> **would shock my eyes**
> **Long used to darkness...**

Again, that's the theme of the "Stranger on the Road" poem. Helen, who is really speaking for all of us, is so identified with the darkness of the ego system that the light of Christ, the light of truth would dissolve, which means that light would dissolve my identity. That's what I strive mightily to preserve.

> **Your light would shock my eyes**
> **Long used to darkness, and to dim effects**
> **That shift like shadows round where someone dies,**
> **And wander back and forth and forth and back**
> **Till light becomes unwanted.**

I don't want the truth any more. I don't want Jesus to appear. I don't want Jesus to be in my life because I cherish my life so much, even in its misery, suffering and death. It is *my* life, it is *my* self, it is *my* body that is suffering and dying. And that's what proves, even in my weakness and my death that I was right and God was wrong. Jesus asks us in the text, "Do you prefer that you be right or happy?" (T-29.VII.1:9). To be right means to be miserable, to be weak, to be separated, to be angry, to be depressed, to be guilty, to feel unfairly treated. We always choose between our weakness and the strength of Christ in us.

> **Did You say** [this is the question to Jesus]
> **That you would never leave me till the end?**
> **Time has no meaning now.**
> **Was it a day,**
> **A month, a year, — eternity, — since You**

Promised to come? [There's that indictment of
Jesus. He did not keep his promises.]
**You said You would redeem
The world. Yet I can only see a cross.
The resurrection seems to be a dream.**

This is the feeling that we all carry with us, but we keep
buried underneath layers upon layers upon layers of specialness. We are always trying to find something in the world
that would satisfy us; something external that would give us
peace: a person, a thought system, *A Course in Miracles*,
anything and everything. Yet underlying all this, *we want
Jesus to fail*. This is a poem that says I don't want your light.
I don't want your resurrection, which the Course defines as
the awakening from the dream of death. I'm perfectly happy
being perfectly miserable living in a place, *a dry and dusty
place where starved and thirsty creatures come to die*.

This is the world of the finite. This is the gory of the finite.
This is the gruesome, painful world that we embrace and that
we call home. This is the place of Holy Saturday. This is an
experience that makes Jesus totally inoperative as a teacher.
This negates him. This says you didn't keep your promises.
You promised me eternal life. You promised me you'd save
the world. And we think of all that as being that he would
grant me eternal life as a person, as an individual; he would
save the world. It's all set up to prove him wrong, to prove
that he's a failure, which means I no longer have to go to him
for help, because I've proven that he's a liar. He doesn't keep
his promises. He doesn't keep his word.

But all that it means is that he's not answered *my question*.
Because the minute I pose my question and express my need
and utter my prayer, I've negated him. Because everything I
utter, no matter how sincere the prayer may be, is all geared
towards something to do with my body, physically or psychologically. It has to do with something in the world, something
external, and not with the mind.

117

It's programming him to fail. It's what he told Helen that by asking him specific questions, she was trying to make his love more manageable. And then he went on, meaning more manageable by you. We're so afraid of his message of Atonement that says the separation never happened; that says you're never upset for the reason you think; that says beyond this world there is a world you want—we're so upset by that that we change him. We crucify him, crucify his course if we're students of *A Course in Miracles*, and in its place raise our special Jesus, who can never make us happy because we don't want to be happy. If we really wanted to be happy, we would not be here.

Why would you choose happiness in *a dry and dusty world where starved and thirsty creatures come to die*? Why would you seek for happiness in the finite? Why would you seek for the glory of the infinite in the finite, in the world of time and space, in the world of bodies? Why would you think that relationships are your salvation, or that a healthy body is your salvation and your peace?

Seek Not Outside Yourself

There's that very important section also in Chapter 29, "Seek Not Outside Yourself." In fact, just let me read something from it. It's page 617, paragraph 2.

(T-29.VII.2:1) No one who comes here but must still have hope, some lingering illusion, or some dream that there is something outside of himself that will bring happiness and peace to him.

That's it. That's everything I've been saying for the last hour. *No one who comes here but must still have hope.* Which means everyone who comes here *still has hope, some lingering illusion, or some dream that there is something outside of himself that will bring happiness and peace to him.*

118

(T-29.VII.3:1-3) The lingering illusion will impel him to seek out a thousand idols, and to seek beyond them for a thousand more. And each will fail him [each special idol will fail you], **all excepting one; for he will die, and does not understand the idol that he seeks is but his death. Its form appears to be outside himself.**

Namely, the body dies. Everyone makes such a big deal about dying, about death. And the reason we do is because we want to make the body the source of the death, and not the thought system that gave rise to the body's dying. It is a thought system that exists only because we believe in it. We make a big deal about birth, we make a big deal about anniversaries of birth, namely birthdays, and we make a big deal about people dying. Analyzing why people die and how they die and (is this right-minded or wrong-minded?)—it misses the whole point. It has nothing to do with the body's death. That's what this is saying.

And each will fail him, [each idol will fail him] *all excepting one; for he will die, and does not understand the idol that he seeks is but his death.* I want there to be death because death proves the ego thought system of separation, sin, guilt and fear is true. And if it's true, I'm true even if my body is dead. That's why the Jesus we embrace is a Jesus of the finite. That Jesus will never lead us to the infinite. Literally, he was made, he was crafted, he was written about to keep us from the infinite and to keep us in the finite. Just read the gospel stories. They're all about the finite. They're all about individuality; they're all about bodies; they're all about sin. They're all about forgiveness of sin, as if sin were something real.

That Jesus will never lead you home. He will lead you more deeply into the finite, as we've seen, and see over and over and over again. What does it mean to be led more deeply into the finite? It means to be more deeply led into the thought system of the finite—separation, sin, guilt, fear, judgment, suffering, pain—all of which then gets projected outside of us so it seems to be outside of our mind.

When we ask help of our internal teacher, we're really asking for help to preserve our finite state. That teacher will succeed admirably, and we'll stay as finite creatures because that's how we set it up. The real teacher, the true Jesus, is beyond the finite. His presence is experienced in the finite, as we'll see in a little while, but his reality is beyond the finite. And he will lead us from the finite to the infinite; from the gore of the finite to the glory of the infinite; from the ego self to the Christ, capital "S" Self. That's the teacher whom we want.

But we won't choose that teacher until we first recognize what this world is like. As Helen and Bill said that fateful afternoon, there must be another way. There must be another teacher. That is why it is so important to understand that any time you attribute any causal power to anything outside of you, outside of your mind, to give you happiness or peace or to bring pain and suffering to you, you are laboring under the wrong assumptions.

You are laboring under the belief that the ego thought system is true and that its teaching will lead you home. Specialness will never lead you home. We desperately need a teacher that is in us but is not of us, meaning not of our ego, who stands beyond that thought system of the finite to speak to us of infinity and then to speak to us how we get there.

Jesus

Let's turn now to Jesus. Let me read something right from the beginning of the text. Page 7 in the text and we'll start in the middle of paragraph 3, sentence 7.

(T-1.II.3:7-13) An elder brother [now here he's speaking of himself, obviously] **is entitled to respect for his greater**

experience, and obedience for his greater wisdom. He is also entitled to love because he is a brother, and to devotion if he is devoted. It is only my devotion that entitles me to yours. There is nothing about me that you cannot attain. I have nothing that does not come from God. The difference between us now is that I have nothing else. This leaves me in a state which is only potential in you.

In other words, we all share the same right mind. We're all cut from the same cloth. We all have the same right mind and we also have an ego. We also have a decision-making self that chooses between the two. Well, Jesus doesn't have an ego, which means there's no longer a decision maker. That's what he means when he says "I have nothing that does not come from God."

(T-1.II.4:1) "No man cometh unto the Father but by me" [that's a scriptural quote, obviously. "No man cometh unto the Father but by me"] does not mean that I am in any way separate or different from you except in time, and time does not really exist.

He's saying, don't make me special. He's saying don't be in awe of me (T-1.II.3:5). You don't stand in awe of someone who's an equal, and I'm an equal. I'm wiser than you because I know that nothing here is real, and that God did not create this world and this body. But I'm no different from you except in time, and time is an illusion.

(T-1.II.4:2-5) The statement ["No man cometh unto the Father but by me"] is more meaningful in terms of a vertical rather than a horizontal axis. You stand below me and I stand below God. In the process of "rising up," I am higher because without me the distance between God and man would be too great for you to encompass. I bridge the distance as an elder brother to you on the one hand, and as a Son of God on the other.

Jesus is the bridge. We need an interim step because we don't go from the finite to the infinite. We made the finite because we were terrified of the infinite. And that terror is still there. We have to gradually erode the fear that the ego has taught us to associate with perfect love. We do that with any means that would lead us to that love such as forgiveness or choosing the miracle. We need a gentle process and we need a gentle hand that guides us, that leads us, that comforts us, that symbolizes what we're not yet ready to accept.

In the end, there is no Jesus any more than there is any individual. But since we live in a split-off fragmented world, we need symbols that represent what we have chosen to forget; what we have chosen to dissociate; what we've chosen to split off from. We need a bridge that seemingly joins us in the illusion and gently leads us out of the illusion to the truth.

Jesus is one name among many, many, many thousands. Choose any symbol that you want. But he's one symbol. As the manual says, "The name of Jesus Christ as such is but a symbol, but it stands for love that is not of this world" (M-23. 4:1). If Jesus is not comfortable for you, choose any other symbol that represents for you a love that is not of this world that is not special; a love that does not believe that 2+2=4 that does not adhere to the laws of this world; a love that does not grant power, causative power to any aspect of the illusion.

Again, give things here no power to make you happy or sad and no power to give you pleasure or pain. We're told twice in "The Obstacles to Peace" pleasure and pain are the same illusion, opposite sides of the same coin, because both serve to make the body real; to make the finite real (T-19. IV-A.17:11; B.12:1). Pleasure says my body is real. Pain says my body is real. Therefore, they're the same, because they share the same purpose.

You want a teacher who is not taken in by the world, who doesn't insist that you do certain things; that you pray certain times each day; that you do anything. Those of you who know your Plato may remember that when Plato talked about the last days of Socrates and Socrates' trial; Socrates speaks in his defense, and he says from the time he was a child, he always heard a voice

That voice *never* told him what to do. It always told him what not to do. In other words, the voice undid his illusions. It did not tell him what to do. Now this was twenty-five hundred years ago.

In the Course, in Chapter 5, which is the first chapter that really talks seriously about the Holy Spirit, Jesus describes the Holy Spirit and says He doesn't command, He doesn't overcome. He simply reminds (T-5.II.7:1-5). He doesn't tell you what to do. Always watch out for that inner voice that tells you what to do. Next time that inner voice tells you what to do, say, "How much is 2+2?" And if the answer is 4, you know where the voice came from. Socrates' voice did not tell him what to do. It stopped him from doing what was of the ego. He didn't say "ego."

You want your figure of Jesus whom you go to for help to help you undo your ego. You want him to help you learn to forgive, to let go of grievances, to let go of your investment in specialness: special love or special hate. You want this inner voice, the same inner voice Socrates heard, to gently guide you through the morass of the ego thought system. How are you guided through this morass? Through this *dry and dusty place where starved and thirsty creatures come to die*? How are you guided through it? You're guided through it by not giving it any power. And then the demons will just fall away. The only power the dream has is the power that you give it.

Our mind made a distinct choice against the glory of the infinite, because our individual self could not exist there. We made a deliberate choice against the glory of the infinite to choose instead the pseudo-glory of the finite: the glory of being an individual, existing, making the thought system of separation alive and well. Then we invented our own teachers and our own god and our own holy, sacred books that support our worship of the finite.

That's not the teacher you want to listen to. You don't want a teacher who makes the finite real and then tells you it's not real. You want a teacher who helps you realize these are the interim steps, the gentle ways. You want a teacher who helps you realize that the finite can't take the peace of God away from you. That's what the Course's Jesus does, as is clearly distinct from the Christian Jesus, the gospel Jesus and the Jesus of tradition.

He helps you realize that nothing here has any power over you. Ultimately, he says, because there's nothing here. But that's not meant to encourage us to deny what our experiences are because that doesn't help. You want an inner teacher who's the bridge between the finite and the infinite, between the pseudo-glory of the ego and the true glory of God and His Son. You want a teacher who will seemingly join you in the illusion and gently let the illusions fade away, helping you recognize the purpose of embracing the illusion, of making a world. It's our fear of the infinite that drives us to embrace the finite. Because there's no way we could even approximate the infinite.

Truth will correct all errors in my mind.

Let me read you something else. This is from the workbook, Lesson 107. I read this every once in a while. I've read this in classes as a way of helping us realize why Jesus doesn't talk very much about what Heaven is like, and what truth is like, and why it is so important that we have a teacher, once again, who represents the infinite, and yet we still experience him within the world of the finite. It's page 192 in the workbook, paragraph 2.

(W-pI.107.2) Can you imagine what a state of mind without illusions is? How it would feel? Try to remember [by the way, when we're talking about a state of mind without illusions, we're talking about a state of mind without specialness, without judgment, without pain, without bodies, without winning or losing. Because all of these are illusory states. How it would feel? Try to remember] **when there was a time,—perhaps a minute, maybe even less—when nothing came to interrupt your peace; when you were certain you were loved and safe. Then try to picture what it would be like to have that moment be extended to the end of time and to eternity. Then let the sense of quiet that you felt be multiplied a hundred times, and then be multiplied another hundred more.**

(W-pI.107.3:1-4) And now you have a hint, not more than just the faintest intimation of the state your mind will rest in when the truth has come. Without illusions there could be no fear, no doubt and no attack [and no individual self]. **When truth has come all pain is over, for there is no room for transitory thoughts and dead ideas to linger in your mind. Truth occupies your mind completely, liberating you from all beliefs in the ephemeral.**

All beliefs in the ephemeral—the ephemeral meaning what doesn't last. One of the important criteria that Jesus uses in Lesson 133, "I will not value what is valueless," how you distinguish between what is of value and what has no value is, is it eternal? Does it last? And if it doesn't, it has no value.

So again, you want a teacher who truly knows the difference between the valuable and the valueless. The only thing of value in this world of illusion is what leads you beyond the illusion. The Course says of the Holy Spirit that He uses time to teach us there is no time. Jesus uses forgiveness, which is an earthly form of love, to teach us there is no earthly form of love. There's only love. Jesus uses himself as a teacher to make himself obsolete; in fact, in the end, to make himself unrecognizable, because he doesn't exist anymore than we exist. But until that time comes when we know we don't exist, we need someone who appears to exist within our dream. But we need to remember he's a symbol.

(W-pI.107.3:4-6) Truth occupies your mind completely, liberating you from all beliefs in the ephemeral. They have

no place because the truth has come, and they are nowhere [meaning all the illusions]. **They can not be found, for truth is everywhere forever, now.**

One of the points that is made in the text which parallels this is that when we're in the real world, we have no memory of anything else. We have no memory of our life here because there is no life here. How could you remember an illusion? When you're in the real world, you're just like one instant away from Heaven. There's nothing left. You know everything here is unreal. So what is there to remember?

I always like to define memory as a present decision projected into a nonexistent past. When I'm in the real world, there's nothing left in me to decide. I don't have a mechanism to decide any more. Once we choose, once and for all, the right mind over the wrong mind, Atonement over separation and have accepted the Atonement for ourselves, there's nothing to correct. There's nothing to be a corrective agent. There's no wrong mind, there's no right mind, there's nothing to choose. There's no decision maker. There's no memory. If memory is a present decision projected into a nonexistent past and there's no longer a decision maker, there can be no memory.

In that image which is used only once in the Course, the carpet of time; in the instant when the separation seemed to happen, the entire carpet of time rolled out (T-13.I.3:5). The entire expanse of time and space spanning billions and billions of years rolled out and in that same instant, rolled back and was gone. So there'll be nothing left to remember.

It's extremely important that we recognize that what it means to choose Jesus as our teacher, what it means to embrace his thought system, *A Course in Miracles* as our pathway home, means to suspend belief in everything we thought was true. There's that wonderful passage in Lesson 189 where we're asked to empty our mind of all thoughts that we ever had about anything, including God. *Everything.*

Empty our mind of everything, good or bad, holy or unholy, and "come with wholly empty hands unto" our God (W-pI. 189.7:5).

It's very helpful to see how we cling to certain illusions. And to believe that *A Course in Miracles* is your way home, that's an illusion too, even though I just said it. It's an illusion too, because there is no *Course in Miracles*, any more than there's a "you," any more than there is a "Jesus." *A Course in Miracles* is simply a projection into form of the right-minded thought system of correction.

You always have to be very careful and wary of forming a special relationship with this course and with its teacher. Remember, the goal of any teacher is to make himself dispensable. That's what the Course says. Jesus wants us to grow up and become like him so he's no longer an older brother. He's our Self. Not our lower case self, but he's our Self, just as we are his Self. But as long as we cling to the finite and mistaking its secret sins and hidden hates as glorious expressions of truth, we need a teacher who represents the truth to us. What this passage I just read from Lesson 107 is saying, is that you can't have a clue as to what Heaven is like, so we need a bridge.

Jesus of the Bible versus Jesus of *A Course in Miracles*

I want to continue talking about Jesus. I've sometimes been accused of taking Jesus away from people. It's almost like saying there's no Santa Claus. I think I've told this story once but I'll tell it again. I guess this pattern of mine started when I was a kid. There was an Italian family living on our block in Brooklyn. Brooklyn was almost all Jewish or all Italian. I think there were a few Irish that kind of snuck in.

There was an Italian family on our block, and they had a son my age, whose name was Nicky. I don't know how old we were, maybe 8 or 9 years old. And they were a Catholic family, Nicky Larusso, I remember. One day, it was Christmastime, and Nicky took me up to his house to see his Christmas tree and whatever gifts he had. And the conversation came around to Santa Claus, which he obviously believed in. And I said, "Oh, come on, Nicky; don't tell me you believe in Santa Claus. There is no Santa Claus." And he was really upset. I don't know whether his parents talked to my parents, but I remember being spoken to about that. Well, not only is there no Santa Claus, but there's no Jesus as the world has typically thought of him. So I have been accused of taking Jesus away from people.

But you don't want to throw the baby out with the bathwater. The Jesus that I take away is really based on the Course's view obviously; there are other ways of looking at Jesus, but this is the Course's way. So it's to really take all the specialness away. As I was saying before the break, the Jesus that the world has worshipped, that the Bible has written about, and twenty-one hundred years of Christian tradition has revered, is someone who is basically a magician. He does things in the world to help us.

Everyone knows about the miracles, "loaves and fishes," and "water into wine," etc. The resurrection is seen as a miracle, his birth is a miracle and his healings were that way. And certainly Christians are urged to pray to him for help. This is magical from the Course point of view, because it has nothing to do with a change of mind. It has only to do with something to do with the body.

Any time you have a core belief that says sin is real, anything you do to undo that sin has to be magic, because there is no sin. All that has to be corrected and undone and healed is the mind's belief in sin, not sin itself. Sin is not an entity in and of itself. It's not a phenomenon within itself. It's simply a belief. And so I usually joke about asking Jesus for parking spaces and that kind of thing.

What's important is to understand where you're really coming from when you ask Jesus for specific help. You're really coming from a place that says the world is real, my body is real, my problems are real, my problems are very problematic to me, and I need help with my problem. Therefore, I go within, and I ask Jesus or the Holy Spirit for help. The correction for that is what is in back of that message Helen received which I cite very, very often.

This happened after the Course was already completed. Helen one day asked Jesus for help in what she should say to someone who was in need of help. And Jesus' answer to her, which really took her by surprise, was that he did not tell her the words at all. Instead, what he said, "Don't ask me what you should say. Ask me, instead, to help you look at this brother through the eyes of peace and not judgment. And then all the help of Heaven and all the angels will come to your aid" (*Absence from Felicity*, p. 381).

What he was clearly saying is, don't ask me to tell you what to do, what to say, because that's not important. Ask me to help you remove—to cite the beginning of the text—the "blocks to the awareness" of my presence (T-in.1:7). When those blocks are gone, then you would automatically know what to say and what to do. That's what was meant by the metaphor "all the help of angels would come to you." Because then the love in you which you would identify with would then tell you what to say or do. This goes to the heart really of what Jesus ought to be for us.

Again, I'm only speaking from the perspective of *A Course in Miracles*. Since we believe we exist, and no matter how many years you study the Course, as long as you think you're studying the Course, you believe you exist, and the "you" that you believe exists is a very special person. You have a personality, you have a body, you have a history, you have a past, and you have an anticipated future. Therefore, as long as that is there, we need a correction, to quote one passage in the Course that meets us in the condition in which we think we are (T-25.I.7:4). And that condition is a dualistic condition of being in the body, of being in a world of time and space, which is inherently illusory. But as long as we think we're here and that we represent the symbol of the ego thought system of separation and specialness, then we need a corresponding symbol that would correct our mistake.

Jesus is such a symbol. And we'll just stay with Jesus for the moment, although again, as I said earlier today, any symbol of a love that's not of this world would work. It doesn't matter whether you give it a name or not. It doesn't matter if you personify it. It doesn't matter if you see it as an energy force or whatever. But it's recognizing a thought system within you that is not your ego. But we'll stick with Jesus for now.

It's very important that you have an experience of a Self that is outside of your ego, who represents your right-minded Self with which you are out of touch. I read to you earlier the line that, "The name of Jesus Christ as such is but a symbol. But it stands for a love that is not of this world" (M-23.4:1-2). That's the love you want to relate to because that's the answer. That's the ultimate answer to every thought that's part of the ego system: separation, attack, sin, guilt, fear, terror, judgment, cruelty, suffering and death. Every aspect of the ego thought system is gently corrected when you bring it to that love.

Since we think we are individuals and the Course is written to us as if we were individuals, then we need an individual who represents the other. And that's what Jesus represents. That Jesus I would never want to take away from anyone, because that's your ticket home. That's your way home; you can't make this journey alone. It's very difficult to make it without some kind of externalization of this figure called Jesus, but it is impossible to make it alone without realizing there is something within your mind that is sane; something within your mind that is strong, not the strength of the world but the strength of Christ; something in your mind that is innocent, something in your mind that knows not of sin, knows not of separation, knows not of anything of the ego system. Since we give ourselves a name, we therefore give this other thought system a name too. And Jesus is that name. I'm certainly not taking that Jesus away from anyone.

Asking Jesus for Help

And I certainly would also encourage people, especially those who are starting out, and that could span ten, fifteen, twenty years that you still find it helpful to ask this figure for external help. At least you're asking the right figure. But as I always emphasize, you don't want to stay there. You don't want to stay with always asking Jesus to solve problems for you here, whether it's something relatively trivial like a parking space, or relatively significant like healing cancer or helping you make a life-changing decision, it doesn't matter. You're still seeing the world as real and Jesus as this magical figure who waves a magic wand and everything is taken care of for you.

It is much more helpful to follow what he told Helen. Don't ask me what you should say or what you should do. Ask me, instead, to help you look at this person or this situation or this event through the eyes of peace and not judgment. That's the real purpose of having this internal teacher.

When we're told, and most students know this line, "Therefore, seek not to change the world, but choose to change your mind about the world," just plug Jesus into that (T-21.in.1:7). Don't ask Jesus to change your world or to guide you to what you should do in this world. Ask him to help you change your mind about the world. That's the Jesus that you want to get close to. That's the love you want to approximate more and more until you become identified with it. It's that love that you want more than anything else.

You want some symbol of a love that is not of this world, because that's the only way you will be lifted out of this world. But he doesn't do the lifting. We do the lifting,

131

because we're the ones who put us in this mess. But we need a guide who shows us how to, step by step, undo the blocks that protect the descent into hell.

In one passage Jesus talks about how the Holy Spirit leads us up the ladder that the separation led us down (T-28. III.1:2). Well, we kind of fell down with a thud. We slid down all the rungs of specialness until we ended up in this world in a body. So we need help to make our way back up the same ladder, to correct all of our mistakes. You can't do this by yourself. When you do it by yourself, you are simply re-enacting the original mistake when we tried to do Heaven by ourselves, and make Heaven by ourselves, which ended up, of course, being the ego thought system and then the phenomenal universe.

This is not something you want to do by yourself. When we're urged over and over again in this course to ask our Teacher for help, which means in the Course's language either the Holy Spirit or Jesus, we're really asked to join with a non-ego part of ourselves. At the very end we will realize that that presence that we call Jesus or the Holy Spirit is an illusion, just as we're an illusion. But that only comes when we have been able to let go of the ego thought system.

We're told over and over again in so many different ways to take Jesus' hand on the journey. This is not a journey that we make alone. Taking his hand on the journey of course, as we all know, means that as we make our way, we have to bring everyone with us—all of our special love and special hate partners; all the people that we've held grievances against; all the people we think have been salvation for us. But you can't do this by yourself.

Our world here and our physical, psychological experience is built on hate and on guilt. I always quote the line, "The world you see is the delusional system of those made mad by guilt" (T-13.in.2:2). Well, we could say the body is a delusional system of those made mad by guilt. Since guilt is what our lives rest on, and guilt is what has motivated us in this world to preserve our special relationships and that's what has guided us through the maze of our special relationships, we need a love that is the answer to that.

In that sense, you could say the Course is a version of bhakti yoga, which is a form of yoga which is really based on loving the guru. And while you could very well do this course without that experience, I think it greatly enhances it. If you can allow yourself to feel that love, the love that we've invested in people or things or substances or achievements, if we redirected that love to this figure that we call Jesus that's what will take us home. That's the end of specialness, because in his love, everyone is included. In the ego's version of love, everyone is excluded except those particular people we want to cannibalize, we want to murder.

But when you allow this love that this figure represents to come into your life more and more, there's nothing comparable to that here. The greatest love experience anyone could have here is just a pale, pale, pale shadow of that love, of feeling a love that is not of this world. Since we identify ourselves with our own identity, it is really important to then shift that identity to another person, to another identity that is not us.

The only Jesus I want to take away from people is the myth, is the illusion, is the specialness one; not the Jesus who lives in our minds as this tremendous expression of God's Love. He's the window home. He's the doorway through which you will pass. You shouldn't be ashamed of your love for him. You shouldn't be ashamed of asking his help that you become more and more like him, and that you look at the world the way he looks at the world; not that you do what he would have done. Because what bodies do is totally irrelevant. You want to look at the world through his eyes, what the Course calls Christ's vision. That's what you want.

What could be a more wonderful experience to have in this world than to feel that love inside you? And then to let that love just pour through you and embrace everyone? Any time that you feel any thought that is not totally loving and peaceful, which means a peace and a love that does not embrace all people, then not only is it expressing your embrace of the finite, it's also expressing your defense against Jesus and his love because it's that love which is so threatening and so frightening. Yet it's so threatening and frightening because it does mean the dissolution of the ego, slowly and gently. You just don't disappear into the Heart of God, but you gradually let go of all of the encumbrances; you let go of all of the blocks to not only the awareness of love's presence but the direct experience of that presence.

"The Resting Place"

I want to read a nice Jesus poem now. As many of you know, because I have discussed this in the past, in 1977 Helen wrote three Valentine Day poems. They're all love poems to Jesus. One of these is what I'll read now is called "The Resting Place." And it's a lovely poem, and it really expresses not only this love, but that this love is the way back.

My arms are open. Come, my Lord, to me
And rest upon my heart. It beats for you
And sings in joyous welcome. What am I
Except your resting place and your repose?

Your rest is mine. Without you I am lost
In senseless wanderings that have no end.
No goal, no meaning, on a road that goes
In twisted byways down to nothingness.

Come now, my Love, and save me from despair.
The Way, the Truth, the Life are with me then.
The journey is forgotten in the joy
Of endless quiet and your kiss of peace.
(*The Gifts of God*, p. 54)

134

Now who in his right mind would not want this experience? And when you do not have this experience, it is because you're not in your right mind. And that you prefer the "senseless wanderings" on a road that has no meaning and no goal, to the road that will lead you home. That's what you have to really see. It would be so incredibly helpful if each and every moment of your day you juxtapose your experiences of living in this world, cherishing all the crumbs of specialness, luxuriating and being justifiably angry, or settling for just a smile from someone as being a wonderful gift, and juxtapose all of that to this experience of love. Because every time you have any feeling other than this, you are defending against that love. That's what is really implicit in this poem; in fact, all the poems; in fact, in the whole Course.

Everything is purposive. Since that love for Jesus and of Jesus and from Jesus is the only reality in this illusory world, then anything else we experience has to be unnatural. And the unnatural just doesn't just happen. The natural happens naturally. The unnatural has to be chosen. And so there's a reason why we choose our fear and our anxiety and our guilt and our anger and our pain and our suffering and our despair and our depression. There's a reason for that. It just doesn't happen. And it happens because we're afraid of this love.

If this last paragraph is true, then nothing else is true. So let me read it again.

> **Come now, my Love, and save me from despair.**
> **The Way, the Truth, the Life are with me then.**
> **The journey is forgotten in the joy**
> **Of endless quiet and your kiss of peace.**

That love is the journey home. So you want to continually compare the journey you're taking, the journey to specialness, through specialness, from specialness, to this journey. And the teacher you've chosen is your guide through your specialness wanderings to this teacher of love. Because this love is not of this world and therefore will help deliver you from this world. In fact, another love poem of Helen's is called "Deliverance."

When I talk a lot about choosing against a 2+2=4 world and choosing instead a 2+2=5 world, what I'm talking about is this love. The 2+2=4 world is the world of specialness, where there are certain laws. There are laws of manipulation, seduction and control that enable us to get what we want from people. Jesus' love is part of a 2+2=5 world because it cuts through everything here. It cuts through all the seeming laws, which means no matter what has gone on in your life, no matter what is going on in your life right now or might yet happen, will mean absolutely nothing when you experience this love, when you realize that he's *the way, the truth and the life*. Then nothing here makes any difference.

In *The Song of Prayer* pamphlet he asks, why would you trade a momentary experience of love that's practically nothing that lasts for a short period of time when you could have this experience of God's Love? But that's what we're always doing. This cuts through everything.

In the latest article I wrote for our newsletter, it was the Christmas article (The Lighthouse, 2010 #4); I said that you should make this Christmas season about Jesus, but not in the traditional sense. To make it about him means that you want to look at the world his way. Every single thing you do you want to compare, is this the way he would see it? Again, we're not talking about behavior or anything external. Is this the way he would look at this person? When you feel angry at someone or excited about being in someone's presence, ask, "Is this the way Jesus would be? Is this the way he would think? Is the way he would look?" Make it about him.

To piggyback on his New Year's resolution for us at the end of Chapter 15 in the text, "Make this year different by making it all the same," meaning you make it all about him (T-15.XI.10:11). And if you make it all about Jesus, everything will be the same. You'll perceive everything as the same. You will make no distinctions. And you would feel that love. And that love would lift you above everything here. As he says in the Course, it'll lift you above the battleground. Why would you not want that? That's the question you should ask yourself? Why would you set that aside and cast it aside for the pettiness of specialness, whether it's special love or special hate? As I was saying earlier, to do that without judgment and without self-condemnation and without guilt, but just say, "Yes, this just shows how insane I am. He's right." Everything he says in the Course about us being insane is right. I'm willing to throw away that love which would lift me above all of my concerns, all of my cares, all of my anxieties for this: the "this" being any crumb of special-ness that the ego throws our way. That's what you want to look at. Because that's the way you get from the finite to the infinite.

Jesus is the great symbol of the glory of the infinite. Well, what is the glory of the infinite? The glory of the infinite is this perfect love and this perfect Oneness. His vision here reflects that perfect love and perfect Oneness, because we then see everyone as the same.

So again, it would be extraordinarily helpful as you prac-tice this day in and day out that you always compare what you're feeling at any given moment with the feeling you could have of that all-encompassing love; that you could actually feel this loving presence of Jesus in your mind and in your heart that would infuse everything in your life. Why would you want anything else but that? That's the question that you have to ask.

The Glory of the Infinite

I want to use this then as a segue into talking now about the glory of the infinite. Let me read something first from the teacher's manual on page 49. This is another of those passages that gives us a hint of what lies ahead. It's the section "What Is Justice?" I'm going to start reading paragraph 2, sentence 5. In this context, justice would be the correction for the ego's injustice.

In the text, when Jesus talks about justice, especially in Chapters 25 and 26, the injustice of the world is one wins, another loses. Injustice is that the bad get punished and the good get rewarded. There's someone who's innocent and someone who's sinful. There's a differentiation. Heaven's justice, as reflected here, is seeing everyone as the same. In other words, just another way of talking about forgiveness. I mention that because that's how the paragraph ends.

(M-19.2:5-9) The path becomes quite different as one goes along. Nor could all the magnificence, the grandeur of the scene and the enormous opening vistas that rise to meet one as the journey continues, be foretold from the outset. Yet even these, who splendor reaches indescribable heights as one proceeds, fall short indeed of all that wait when the pathway ceases and time ends with it. But somewhere one must start. Justice is the beginning.

In other words, the way we get from here to there, to these glorious vistas that will open up is to practice day in and day out, justice; which means seeing everyone as the same. And again, we need a teacher for that. We need an internal symbol to which we always bring our feelings of injustice. What are the telltale signs? Anytime you divide up the Sonship or fragment the Sonship. As I was saying earlier, any time you give anything in the world; a person, a place, a thing, a substance—the power to affect you.

The "you," of course, is not your body because bodies clearly are affected here. But the "you" is the mind. Nothing can take the love and the peace of God away from you but your decision. Nothing can banish Jesus from your kingdom, the kingdom of your mind, except your decision. But you have to want his vision, you have to want his presence, you have to want his love above everything else. You have to want it.

This is a course in motivation. You have to want this. If you're not motivated, you're not going to learn it, which means when you don't learn this course, it's because your motivation is weak. Learning this course means to look at the world as Jesus does. You walk this world the way he does. And if he's not a meaningful symbol for you, use any other symbol. But it has to be a symbol of a love that is non-special that never has any judgment in it; that doesn't separate out one part of the Sonship from another.

If we really want to begin to experience *the magnificence and the grandeur of the scene and the enormous opening vistas that rise to meet us as the journey continues*, then we have to practice this. If we really want to reach the *splendor that reaches indescribable heights*, and yet even these don't hold a candle to that experience of the glory of the infinite; if that's where we want to go, then Jesus is the man. Jesus is the symbol that will take us there if we do what he says.

This is not a magical Jesus. This is not vicarious salvation or vicarious forgiveness. This is something that we have to grow into and become like him. We have to see the world the way he does, which means we do not make the superficial, and everything here is superficial, differences significant.

In other words, we have to make God's Love the only goal. There's a later workbook lesson, God is the only goal I have today. "Let me remember that my goal is God" (W-pII. 258). But that's not meant in some abstract way or some kind of magical, mystical way. If God is my only goal, then I must choose the means that will help me achieve that goal. And I must choose the teacher whose loving guidance will lead me to that goal. God's Love is perfect Oneness, and in this world that's reflected in perfect sameness: everyone is seen as the same. When we say that *the name of Jesus Christ is a symbol but it's a symbol for a love that is not of this world*, then that's Heaven's Love.

The Father's Love

What I want to do now for the rest of the time is to read from the end of "The Gifts of God." That's the last section called *The Father's Love*. I'm not going to read the whole section but I'll read parts of it. A lot of it I'll just read straight through. Other times I'll read it with you and comment on it. For those of you who are not familiar with "The Gifts of God," just let me talk very, very briefly about it. This is the prose poem that is part of the book called *The Gifts of God* which has Helen's poetry. This is basically the last thing that Helen scribed that I think is legitimate. It was in 1978 when it was completed; Helen died in 1981. She really did very little scribing after this prose poem and a lot of that was very much colored by the deterioration of her own body. But this was the last thing that she took down. It was not meant to be anything other than a series of messages to her at a time when she was very, very frightened. I'll just mention what happened very, very quickly because I don't want to spend too much time on it.

It had to do with me. I used to go once a month to a convent. It was called Maryknoll in Ossining, New York. It was a cloister of nuns and I would go Sunday morning early. I would take the train and I would then go to Mass with the sisters. I was acting like a good Catholic boy. I would meet with a lot of the sisters throughout the day and the next day, and then I'd give a talk to the sisters. I did this every month. Helen knew the sisters, knew a lot of them well and liked the idea that I was going.

Except this one time, there was a snowstorm. It was not snowing when I was leaving. And I had already canceled the previous week because Helen was concerned about the weather, and I couldn't really do it again. The morning that I left, everything was fine. But there was a snowstorm that was predicted and it came, and it was a real blizzard. Helen was frantic and called me all the time. Now I was very safe. The place was warm; there was lots of food. The nuns take very, very good care of you. But she was frantic. The problem was that the switchboard closed down at 10 o'clock. From 10 o'clock on, until the next morning, she could not contact me. And she would always call me. So this was the problem. It was in the state of that high anxiety, which really was over nothing, but for her it was not trivial, that "The Gifts of God" began. I think it was February when it started. But then it continued. The part I'm reading to you now was written in April of 1978, which is when it was completed. Well, when it was all done, the series of seemingly discrete messages really formed a unity.

I've done workshops on the entire "The Gifts of God." It presents a wonderful summary of the entire Course from beginning to end. And it closes, as every part of the Course closes, with a very beautiful, if not rhapsodic conclusion that's very inspiring. This last section is called *The Father's Love*. That's what I'm going to read from.

Interestingly enough, in January of that year, Helen had taken down a personal message. I think it was four paragraphs that fit very nicely into this section that she took down in April. When we decided after Helen died to publish the poetry, I also wanted to publish "The Gifts of God" as an appendix to it. And then I put those four paragraphs in the context of this section. Actually, it's practically seamless; you couldn't even tell. It was almost like it was part of the same dictation, but it just happened in different places. I'll read part of that too. I want to start, then, with *The Father's Love*. For those of you who have the book, it's page 126.

There is a secret place in everyone in which God's gifts are laid, and his to Him.

Now what's interesting about this is that in the Course when the term "secret place" or "secret dream" or "secret" occurs, it's always of the ego. That's the ego thought system that we try to keep secret and hidden in the mind and then project it out, and that's what made the world and sustains the world. Here it's used really to talk about the right mind. Instead of the secret place being the wrong-minded thought system of separation and guilt and hate, here it's the place where the memory of God is kept for us.

In the metaphoric language of the Course, that's what the Holy Spirit does. He is that memory of love, and He holds it for us in our right minds until the time comes that we can choose it. This is the secret place, which really is the guiding metaphor of this closing section.

There is a secret place in everyone in which God's gifts are laid, and his to Him.

And these gifts, of course—and the title of this is "The Gifts of God"—would be the gifts of love, the gifts of Oneness, the gifts of eternal life, the gifts of the glory of the infinite. These gifts are in all of us.

It is not secret to the eyes of Christ Who sees it plainly and unceasingly.

It's not hidden. When we're in our right minds, we are that. Going back to Jesus, Jesus is the personification, is the great symbol of that love that we have kept buried. And it's because we kept it buried that we need an external symbol. We need a symbol of a seemingly external presence that would lead us there. In truth, of course, we are that gift of God. We are that love.

And we are the ones who lead ourselves to it simply by changing our minds. We chose to keep that secret and walled off, like a secret wall, and in exchange we adopted the ego's special love, the ego's gifts: the gifts of fear, the gifts of attack, gifts of separation, the gifts of specialness.

We're the ones who wandered away into the far country of the ego; therefore, we're the ones who have to change our minds and wander back. But because we don't think we're minds, we think we are bodies, we think we are personalities, once again, we need a symbol that is not us, that seems to be external, who will lead us back. And Jesus is the name of that guide that really is ourselves, but at this point, we don't know that.

Yet it is hidden [yet the secret place is hidden] **to the body's eyes, and to those still invested in the world and caring for the petty gifts it gives, esteeming them and thinking they are real.**

What keeps that secret place hidden, what keeps God's Love away from us, is all our investments in the world: the "caring for the petty gifts" of specialness, the little crumbs that the ego offers us, the seeming pleasures of the body that we would die for or kill for. These are all so insignificant when you compare them to this Love. They are so insignificant when you compare them to the love that Jesus represents. But we can't do that if we're not aware of it.

In the Course we're told that the Holy Spirit teaches through contrast and He is always contrasting two thought systems. We are asked to always contrast these two forms of love: the ego's special love and this love that Jesus holds out to us. While we are invested in the world we won't know that because it's hidden to the body's eyes.

William Blake: "The Everlasting Gospel"

I want to read something. I quote very often, William Blake's idea about not believing the lie. Several years ago I did a workshop on that. I read this to you then, but let me read it again. These are six lines from a much longer poem by William Blake, who was an early nineteenth century great, great poet and visionary. It's called *The Everlasting Gospel*. This same idea appears elsewhere in Blake, but this I think is the clearest statement of it. And it parallels what I just read to you.

> **This life's five windows of the soul**
> **Distorts the Heavens from pole to pole,**
> **And leads you to believe a lie**
> **When you see with, not thro', the eye**
> **That was born in a night, to perish in a night,**
> **When the soul slept in the beams of light.**

This life's five windows of the soul are the five senses that *distorts the Heavens from pole to pole*. This is the exact opposite of Heaven, just as we were discussing at the beginning today. It's our five senses, it's our bodies, it's our brain that takes all the input, all the sensory data that our sensory organs bring to us and puts them in a picture. As the Course explains in many other places, the picture the brain puts it in is what the mind tells it to do; i.e., that the world is real. There's a world out here that with the five senses I can see, I can hear, I can touch, I can feel, I can taste with five senses. The *five windows of the soul distorts the Heavens from pole to pole*.

These five senses, i.e., the body, which means the ego thought system in the mind that made the body for this purposes; they lead *you to believe a lie when you see with, not thro', the eye*. What Blake is talking about here is exactly what the Course is talking about. When we see with the eyes, we see a world out here and we believe it. When we see through the eyes, we're looking beyond the sensory world. We're looking beyond the phenomenal universe. We're going back to the thought beyond the form. We're choosing the content instead of the form. We're choosing our teacher, the Jesus of love, rather than the Jesus of special love. Not a Jesus who tells us how to live in this world; but a Jesus who tells us that the world is not real. And he teaches us how to use the world and our experiences in this world as a way to lead us beyond the world and take us home.

These five senses lead us *to believe a lie when we see with, not through* the eye. And the eye, the sensory world *was born in a night, to perish in a night.* The night being the world of the ego: *when the soul slept in the beams of light.* Here we have this light all around us and we still choose to remain asleep. And it's our sensory apparatus that is the mechanism that the ego uses. The problem is not with our bodies or our sensory organs or the brain that interprets all the data. The problem is that we choose a teacher in the mind that makes all this real to us.

The Father's Love (cont.)

Getting back now to "The Gifts of God."

Yet [the secret place] **is hidden to the body's eyes...**

Which means the body will never see it. The reason I continue to contrast the Jesus of the Bible with the Jesus of *A Course in Miracles* is the Jesus of the Bible makes sin real and therefore, makes the world of bodies real. I don't care how you want to reinterpret the Bible, that's where it's coming from. Sin is real, the world is real, bodies are real, problems are real here. Go out and preach to the masses and convert them.

The Jesus in the Course would say "What masses? There's only one person you have to convert: *you.* There's only one problem you have to solve and heal: your mind's belief in separation. There's only one love in this world and it's not in this world." So again, the secret place where God's Love:

...is hidden to the body's eyes, and to those still invested in the world and caring for the petty gifts it gives, esteeming them and thinking they are real.

This is all about specialness, without the word being used. This is accepting and wanting and cherishing and coveting the loves of this world, rather than the love that Jesus holds out to us. If you really want to awaken from the dream and return home and disappear into the Heart of God, which is the Heart of His Love, then you have to look at all of the special ways you have substituted for that love and say, "*I don't want this anymore.*" You must do that. Not that you have to do it perfectly. Not that you even let it go, but you have to begin to experience the motivation to let it go.

Jesus is asking us to grow up and become like him: to enter into this secret place so that it's not a secret any more. Wasn't there a song Doris Day sang long ago, "My Secret Love is No Secret Any More" or something like that? Well, this is our real secret love. It's not a special love. Jesus represents that love for us and symbolizes that love. When you feel his presence, you would just go right beyond it. You would look into his eyes and you would pass beyond the eyes. You don't look at the eyes. You look through the eyes. And looking through his eyes means you're looking through the eyes of vision. These are the eyes that will take you home. Why would you want anything else?

The "petty gifts" that the ego offers us is not only the gifts of special love, not only the gifts of having all your needs met. It's also the gifts of pain and suffering and justified anger and hurt. Remember, there's no difference between pleasure and pain, because they serve the same purpose. And when that makes you angry, it's only because you are cherishing the body. Don't take my body away from me. Don't take my specialness away from me.

There's nothing here, so the only thing that gives meaning to our perception that things are here is purpose. Pleasure and pain are the same because they serve the same purpose of making the body real. This makes no sense to a body but it makes absolute sense to a mind that wants to change itself, and wants to hear the call of love for love and say yes, I want to return home. Then everything I do from that moment on would be geared towards achieving that goal.

It doesn't mean I would be ego free. It simply means I would see any ego reaction as a classroom in which I can learn the lesson *to see not with my eye but through my eye*; not look at the world through the eyes of 2+2=4, but looking at the world from the perspective of 2+2=5. That's the only thing that gives life meaning here.

Read the early workbook lessons. Nothing in this room means anything (W-pI.1). I have given the meaning to everything that's here. It means nothing because I gave it my ego's purpose. Why would you do that? That's what Jesus is saying: "How long, O holy Son of God? How long?" (W-pII. 4.5:8). *How long?* How much longer are you going to wait, to punish yourself? Don't be stubborn. Stubbornness is only fear. And you're only afraid of me. How could you be afraid of me? I represent the Love of God. Why else would you study my course unless you wanted to return home? This is how you do it.

This doesn't mean that you don't have ego thoughts. It means you don't justify them. You don't argue for them. You don't seek to reinforce them. You simply say yes, I got a little insane. I became afraid of love again, and I saw Jesus as my enemy. I saw him as this ogre. I saw him as this tyrant who's demanding I be a certain way, when all he's doing is gently reminding me, choose again and choose me. Why would you not choose my love as your truth? Why? That's what all this is saying.

Illusions' gifts [again, think of all the gifts of specialness] **will hide the secret place where God is clear as day, and Christ with Him.**

This is purpose. The word isn't used here but this is purpose: to see illusions' gifts have as their purpose to hide the secret place. And to see how we take the substitutions of special love for Heaven's Love, for Jesus' love. Why do this? And that's what the next sentence says.

O let this not be secret to the world so full of sorrow and so racked with pain. You could relieve its grief and heal its

pain, and let the peace of God envelop it as does a mother rock a tired child until it sighs and slips away to rest.

He's not talking about healing the world out there and bringing rest to all the people who are tired out there. He's talking about bringing rest to your own tiredness, the tiredness of fighting against reality, of fighting against this love. When you give that up and you embrace his love, then that love will just naturally embrace everyone because minds are joined. The text says, "Minds are joined; bodies are not" (T-18.VI.3:1). *Minds are joined. Bodies are not.*

This love that you now accept would embrace everyone. Just as we're told in the Course that we were with Jesus when he arose, when he awakened from the dream of death, which has nothing to do with the gospel myths—*nothing* to do with that. When he awoke from the dream of death, we were with him because there's only one Son and minds are joined. We keep separating ourselves from that love.

And again, the great, great tragedy of what Christianity did is they made Jesus into a body. They made salvation into a bodily act. How insane is that? It's not the body that's the problem. The body is not the locus of sin. It's the mind. *Resurrection is a change of mind.* How could the body rise and ascend to Heaven? It never fell.

What could have been taken as a great myth became taken as history and theological truth that people killed for and killed over. He's pleading with us, *O let this not be secret to the world.* Don't let my love be secret. And again, you can see the distortion. He's not asking us to stand on street corners and proclaim that Jesus is Lord. He's not saying when you score a winning touchdown that you look up to Heaven and thank God for it and praise Jesus. He's not talking about making a public spectacle of yourself. He's talking about embracing that love in your heart and in your mind. And then that love will dictate what you'll say and do, and you'll have no investment in what you say and do.

O let this not be secret to the world so full of sorrow and so racked with pain.

And we are that world.

We'll skip a paragraph.

O be at peace, beloved of the Lord! [That's us, and the Lord is God here.] **What is your life but gratitude to Him Who loves you with an everlasting Love? What is your purpose here but to recall into His loving Arms the Son He loves, who has forgotten Who his Father is?**

What is your life? What is the meaning of our life but being grateful for Who we really are? And then letting that gratitude be directed towards our teacher who will lead us home. That's the only meaning. *What is your life?* What is the meaning of your life except to feel this gratitude? *What is your purpose here* but to remember these loving Arms? That's what you want to see.

Your purpose is not to have a great life here. That doesn't mean you should have a terrible life here. It just means what life here? This is so clear. *What is your purpose here but to recall into His Loving Arms the Son He loves, who has forgotten Who his Father is?* Well, how do we remember Who God is? How do we remember that love? We learn how to express it here by seeing everyone as the same. We live our lives here as a reflection of that love with the Teacher who is the reflection of that love.

And so again, what you want to do is continue to juxtapose the pettiness of your thoughts that are so trivial and insignificant when you place them next to this magnificence, this glorious glory of the infinite. It's so trivial. It's not trivial from the point of view of the body. But as I always say, don't believe anyone who tells you 2+2=4. They don't know. They think things here are important. They think feelings are important, for God's sake. Everyone makes a big deal about feelings. I have this feeling. Yes, the problem is that *you* have this feeling. You as a person have a feeling; that won't get you home. Do you want to match your feeling with the feeling of love? You want to use whatever you experience here as a way to get home. *What is your purpose here but to recall into His Loving Arms the Son He loves, who has forgotten Who his Father is?* That's your purpose. You see everything here as now designed by this Teacher—he didn't choose it, but he now gives it a different purpose—as a way to remind you of Who you are.

If you are a Child of perfect love and perfect Oneness, then the reflection of that principle is to see everyone here as the same. And just be aware when you're angry or you're jealous or you're competitive or you're depressed or despairing, you have made a conscious choice to push this purpose out of your awareness. And look at that with open eyes but without guilt or without judgment, but look at it.

What is your only goal, your only hope, your only need, the only thing you want, but to allow the secret place of peace to burst upon the world in all its joy, and let the Voice within it speak of Him Whose love shines out and in and in-between, through all the darkened places to embrace all living things within its golden peace?

That's a long sentence. That was one sentence I read you. *What is your only goal, your only hope, your only need* but this? The only hope, the only goal, the only need you have is to open up that secret place of peace and let it shine throughout and *embrace all living things within its golden peace.* Let that be your ideal. Let that be the first thought you have when you open your eyes in the morning; that this is what I want to dedicate my day to. I want to do whatever it is that would undo the obstacles to opening this secret place.

I assure you, if that is what your goal is, you won't covet and cherish all your pettiness: all those little grievances and thoughts of anger and being unfairly treated or getting excited about a person. They will all really be so reduced in size and so insignificant that you would never again tolerate yourself thinking these were important; if you could open every day with this thoght.

What is your only goal, your only hope, your only need, the only thing you want, but to allow the secret place of peace to burst upon the world in all its joy, and let the Voice within it speak of Him Whose love shines out and in and in-between, through all the darkened places to embrace all living things within its golden peace? Who would ever want anything but this? This is why you're all students of this book. In the end, this is what you want. And then see how quickly you dissociate it and split it off and forget, and go back to the trivial pursuits of the insignificant.

There's that wonderful phrase in the workbook; we're going to do a class on later next year: "the thunder of the meaningless" (W-pI.106.2:1). *The thunder of the meaningless.* That's what all this is. When we're interested in the thunder of the meaningless, we don't hear that still, small voice speak to us of God's Love. We don't feel Jesus' gentle presence and his gentle touch on our shoulder that says, my brother, choose again. Look at this differently. What are you going to gain by being right? What are you going to gain by seducing, controlling, manipulating, cannibalizing someone or something out there for a moment's ecstasy? Is that worth throwing away again the Love of God?

That doesn't mean not to enjoy things here, but keep them within perspective. It doesn't mean not to feel pleasure here. It doesn't mean to become an ascetic and deny things here. But it does mean put everything in perspective. Your goal is God. Your goal is to return Home. Your goal is to open up all the darkened places, all the spots of darkness, all the spots of guilt and hate buried in your mind, and undo them by simply bringing them to this love. That's the role of Jesus in our Atonement path, to be the love and the light to which, to whom we bring all of our darkened thoughts. But you have to bring them to him. This is not magic. You don't turn them over in a magical way. You have to look at them with him.

When he tells us that we join with him and we look at the ego so we see beyond it, it's what William Blake was talking about. You don't look with the eye. You look through the eye. You use all your sensory impressions and what your brain does with those impressions to go beyond it, instead of making it real; and again, coveting it and cherishing it.

At this point, is where we put that special message that Helen took down in January of 1978. Let me read you one paragraph of that.

Do not imagine He will leave [the "He" being God] **His child who heard His Voice and listened to His Word. Remember this: The thanks of God are yours and will not leave you comfortless for long. You still are needed in the world, to hear His Voice and share His messages of love with those who call in sorrow. Could it be that you will fail to find Him, when His need for you becomes as great as yours for Him? You need not fear that you will suffer loss, nor that He will abandon you who gave His comfort to His Son. Receive the gift you gave to God and He would give to you.**

This gift, again, is God's Love. We have as our goal learning that God did not abandon us, Jesus did not abandon us; we abandoned Them. That's what the beginning of this paragraph means. *Do not imagine He will leave His child who heard His Voice and listened to His Word.* He did not abandon us. We believe we abandoned Him, and then we project that out.

That's why when we made our dream here and wrote our scripts, a major theme in almost everyone's ego script is that we've been abandoned, we've been rejected, we've been betrayed. People are unkind, are insensitive. And we want to have this, which is why we continually experience it, because this is how we let ourselves off the hook. I did not abandon

God. He abandoned me. I did not abandon this person; he or she abandoned me.

Now this doesn't justify other people's egos. It just makes the point, which is made over and over again; their egos have nothing to do with me unless I give them power over me. How can your dream affect me? I'm the dreamer of my dream. But I use your dream as a way of reinforcing the ego's secret dream that I'm the one who abandoned God. I'm the one who betrayed Him. And then I flip it around through projection: He abandoned me.

The poem I read to you earlier, "Holy Saturday," is basically Helen's not-so-veiled attack on Jesus, "You didn't keep your promise." Well, the guilt is, she didn't keep hers. We haven't kept ours. We abandoned him and his love. The gospel stories of betrayal: Peter betrayed Jesus three times, Judas betrayed him. This is everyone's story. That's why these stories have such a hold on us. It's not because they're real or true, but because they speak to the guilt in all of us.

We're the silent betrayers. We're the ones who turn away from love. Every time we cherish any unkind thought and justify any unkind behavior or unkind words, we are betraying that love again. We're telling Jesus and telling God as we all did at the beginning, "Your love is not enough." And he's pleading with us: "Why keep doing this? Enough already. *How long, O holy Son of God, how long?* Why are you going to continue to keep Heaven away?"

Twice he says in the Course, "Why wait for Heaven?" (W-pI.131.6:1; 188.1:1). Heaven is right here. I'm right here, Jesus says. But every time you have an unkind thought, anytime you have a thought that differentiates among the Sonship, it's a decision to push that love away. And rather than accept responsibility for it, we project it out and we make up all kinds of stories and get lots of people to agree with us; people did unconscionable things to me. They didn't do unconscionable things to you. They did them to themselves. What do you have to do with it?

153

That's why I always emphasize you can't understand this course, let along practice it and live it, if you keep the metaphysics hidden. You always have to bring the metaphysics right there with you. What does your dream have to do with me, unless I give it power to, unless I join with your dream? Then I'm as insane as you are, and I'm as cruel as I accuse you of being.

We're coming now to the last two paragraphs of "The Gifts of God." What's interesting here is that the voice suddenly changes. Instead of Jesus talking to us, it's now God Himself talking to us. Now this is just stylistic. God doesn't speak any more than Jesus speaks. But this is the end of the whole sequence of these "Gifts of God" messages, and of the section called (we actually called it—Helen didn't give it any names), *The Father's Love*. So now this is God speaking.

You are My Son, and I do not forget the secret place in which I still abide, knowing you will remember.

You are My Son, and I do not forget the secret place in which I still abide. I'm still there. I have not left. Jesus has not left. The Holy Spirit has not left. You left. And the "you" is the decision-making self. That is so important to not only understand intellectually, but to really see how that works in your own life.

No one, *absolutely no one*, no circumstance, no event can take the peace and the Love of God away from you. You should brand that on your forehead and put it on your mirrors and your refrigerators. Nothing in this world can take the Love and peace of God away from you, because there's no world outside of your mind. It's your mind. Once again, contrast that truth with what you've made to be your truth.

I was feeling very happy until this person did or said whatever he or she said and did. That's a lie. Don't believe the lie. Remember, that's what Blake said. "This life's five windows of the soul distorts the Heavens from pole to pole, and leads you to believe a lie when you see with, not thro', the eye."

Don't believe your senses and don't believe your brain that interprets all these sensory data. Don't believe them. It's not true. No matter what goes on in the world, you have the power of your mind to remain fully embracing of that love. The secret place is secret because we closed the door and then forgot about it. The purpose of *A Course in Miracles* is to help us remember that we closed it and how painful it has made our lives ever since then, collectively as well as individually. That's the cause of our pain. Putting God's Love in this secret place and locking the door. Remember how "Holy Saturday" began, Helen's poem. "The door is solid," and I'll never penetrate it. But it's nothing. I put it there and it's nothing. In one passage in the text (T-18.IX.6:4) Jesus says, does a cloud have the power to hold a button? It doesn't. The clouds of guilt have no power. The doorway of guilt has no power.

So again, God says:

You are My Son, and I do not forget the secret place in which I still abide, knowing you will remember. Come, My Son, open your heart and let Me shine on you, and on the world through you.

Come, My Son, open your heart and let Me shine on you, and on the world. It's our responsibility. It's our doing. God can't do it. We open that secret place. We bring our fear to that Love. We bring our defenses to that Love and the door is open. Light abolishes the darkness. Love abolishes fear.

The famous passage from John's first epistle which is quoted in the first chapter of the text, "*Perfect love casts out fear*" (T-1.VI.5:4). In the presence of love, there can't be any fear, which means if there's fear or any other aspect of the ego thought system, it's purposive to keep love away from us.

You are My light [this is God speaking to us] **and dwelling place. You speak for Me to those who have forgotten. Call them now to Me, My Son, remember now for all the world.**

155

There's that word "all" again. *Call them now to Me, My Son, remember now for all the world.* One could see this course as a way of helping us hear that call and answer it. Since minds are joined, when we answer it that love not only floods through our mind, it floods through the mind of the Sonship as another reminder to everyone they can choose again.

Remember the passage I mentioned earlier where Jesus says how the Holy Spirit doesn't command; He doesn't overcome; He simply reminds (T-5.II.7:1-4). And as His manifestation in the world, just as Jesus was His manifestation in the world, we remind each other by our defenselessness and our love that must be born of our experience. If we don't experience that love, then all we're doing is we're just talking words. And no one listens to words. They always hear what's underneath the words. If you're talking the words, but there's no love underneath, then that's what people will hear. They'll hear the sham. They'll hear the specialness. They may like it because it feeds their specialness, and then you both do this dance of death and participate in it.

I call in love, as you will answer Me, for this the only language that we know. Remember love, so near you cannot fail to touch its heart because it beats in you.

Again, this is the exhortation to us: *Remember love.* Well, you can't remember love if you've chosen to forget it and have chosen instead to remember special love. I always say that there's nothing positive in this course. It's always the undoing of the negative. That's what's positive. We have to forget what we remembered, which is the ego's version of love, and remember Heaven's Love that we forgot. And that's what this is a call to.

Remember love, so near you cannot fail to touch its heart because it beats in you. Do not forget. Do not forget, My child. Open the door before the hidden place, and let Me blaze upon a world made glad in sudden ecstasy.

Open the door before the hidden place, and let Me blaze upon a world made glad in sudden ecstasy. That's the call. *Open the door.* We closed it. I don't usually cite the Bible, but there's one passage in the gospels where Jesus says, "Lo I stand at the door and knock. Let he who hear open the door." Now he doesn't break the door down. *A Course in Miracles* would be Jesus knocking. He's knocking on the doorway to our mind and saying, open it to me. That's what this is saying. In the Person of God, God is saying, open the hidden place.

Why would you not? That's the question. Why would I not open it? Why would I settle for so little? That's why having a relationship with Jesus or some other symbol is so important, because that's what would lead you to that experience. Once you have even a glimmering of experiencing that love, you wouldn't settle for anything else here. And when you do, it would hurt you. You would just feel it inside. Why do I keep doing this? Why do I keep pushing love away? But you have to be aware that you push it away and that you no longer want to.

The next sentences, I want to give a little explanation of them. The last phrase I read was *a world made glad in sudden ecstasy.* What I'm going to read you now has this kind of ecstatic flavor to it and it comes from something Helen really loved. Helen always liked Vivekananda, who was the disciple of Ramakrishna. They were both very, very advanced beings in the late nineteenth and early twentieth century. Ramakrishna was this Indian guru who was basically illiterate. He had a circle of people who venerated him. Vivekananda was his chosen disciple to the West. Vivekananda was sent to England to learn English and to study Western thought. He came to the United States in 1893 to speak to a congress of religions in Chicago. And he stood everyone on their ear. He had a tremendous impact.

Ramakrishna's wife, Sri Sarada Devi, was called Holy Mother. She survived Ramakrishna by many, many years.

Many people who knew them both really thought she was even holier than Ramakrishna. Vivekananda would check in with her from time to time. She was in India, and he would write her letters. Some of those letters are absolutely beautiful and very rhapsodic and ecstatic of his love for her. In one of them he said, "I come, Mother, I come." That's what this is based on now. Let me read the phrase just before it.

...let Me blaze upon a world made glad in sudden ecstasy. I come, I come. Behold Me. I am here for I am You; in Christ, for Christ, My Own beloved Son, the glory of the infinite, the joy of Heaven and the holy peace of earth, returned to Christ and from His hand to Me.

This is what we turn against. That's what we have to see. It's this ecstatic love that just dissolves the world and all of our specialness and all of our concerns, that's what we have to choose.

Say now Amen, My Son,

Most of you know the story that when Helen was laboring under taking down the Course, the text was going on and on and on (three years), she said, isn't this damn thing finished yet? And Jesus said, "You will know it's finished when you hear the word 'Amen.'" All the books end with "Amen," and this ends that way too.

Say now Amen, My Son, for it is done. The secret place is open now at last. Forget all things except My changeless Love. Forget all things except that I am here.

I want to close by rereading those last two paragraphs, but this is the call. And what you really want to do is lift yourself above the daily humdrum existence that we all live in, but not to deny what you have to do. We all have to eat and we have to take care of ourselves and our loved ones and all the things that we're familiar with. But you want to put them in perspective. See them as stepping stones towards helping us get back to that secret place and open the door. That's what you want.

Why settle for all the petty things that we get so concerned about? All the anxieties and the angers and the grievances and the special love expectations; they're not worth anything when you put them next to this love. That's what you want. That's what this is a plea to do. It was not just a plea to Helen. It's a plea to all of us. That's why we published it. It's a plea to open the secret place that we have put this love and barricaded ourselves against it and settled for so, so little—all the very shabby substitutes. In the Course, Jesus refers to the body and the ego as a travesty and a parody of the glorious Self that God created (T-24.VII.10:9; W-pI.95.2:1). This is a plea to us to really hear the call of the glory of the infinite and say, "I don't want all the pseudo-glories of this world. I want the truth, I want reality and I want this love."

Let me read the end of this straight through now. And this is a call, again, from God to us.

You are My Son, and I do not forget the secret place in which I still abide, knowing you will remember. Come, My Son, open your heart and let Me shine on you, and on the world through you. You are My light and dwelling place. You speak for Me to those who have forgotten. Call them now to Me, My Son, remember now for all the world. I call in love, as you will answer Me, for this the only language that we know. Remember love, so near you cannot fail to touch its heart because it beats in you.

Do not forget. Do not forget, My child. Open the door before the hidden place, and let Me blaze upon a world made glad in sudden ecstasy. I come, I come. Behold Me. I am here for I am You; in Christ, for Christ, my Own beloved Son, the glory of the infinite, the joy of Heaven and the holy peace of earth, returned to Christ and from His hand to Me. Say now Amen, My Son, for it is done. The secret place is open now at last. Forget all things except My changeless Love. Forget all things except that I am here.

Made in the USA
Las Vegas, NV
18 March 2025

19743010R00095